With best regards
from
Anne Hulbert
26ª September 1991.

# MACHINE
# QUILTING
## —AND—
# PADDED WORK

# MACHINE QUILTING
## — AND —
# PADDED WORK

B.T. Batsford Ltd, London

*To Denis*

First published 1991
© Anne Hulbert 1991

Typeset by Servis Filmsetting Ltd, Manchester
and printed in Great Britain by The Bath Press, Avon

Published by
B.T. Batsford Ltd
4 Fitzhardinge Street
London W1H 0AH

A catalogue record for this book is available from the British Library

ISBN 0 7134 3662 X

# Contents

# Acknowledgements

The author would like to offer her warmest thanks and appreciation to the following for their contribution to the production of this book – and, not least, for their patience in waiting so long for its appearance.

For allowing their work to be photographed for publication: Jackie Anderson; Pauline Burbidge; Manuel Canovas; Kim Clarke; Jacky Cook; Anna Donovan; Barbara Duncan; Dylon International Ltd; Valerie Hadley; Diana Harrison; Claire H. Johnson; Glenys Massey; Karen McCormac; Nicky Mills; Anne Murray; Kate O'Neill; Sally-Ann Ousley; Vivien Prideaux; Sue Rangeley; Phyllis Ross; Diana Thornton.

For producing the line drawings: Anna Donovan; Denis Hulbert; Rosemary Muntus; Dover Publications Inc; William Briggs & Co. Ltd (Deighton's Transfers).

For photographing the work: Toni Carver; Bob Croxford; Rebecca Ross; Peter Tebbitt; Keith Tidball; Chris Upton; Terry Waddington.

For their help and support: Buzz Baker and the staff at The Arcade Sewing Machine Company, Broadmead, Bristol; Anne Harris of The World of Sewing (expert adviser and demonstrator of Bernina sewing machines, accessories and techniques); Anne Morell; Eirian Short.

For supplying materials and equipment, and providing helpful advice: Automative Chemicals for CarPlan spray paints (ozone-friendly); Bogod Machine Co. for Bernina Sewing Machines; Coates for threads and yarns; Deka for textile paints; Dewhurst for sewing threads and requisites; Dylon International for textile paints; Freudenberg Nonwovens for Vilene & Bondaweb; Newey Goodman Ltd for sewing requisites; HomeStyle for spray paints (ozone-friendly); Lowe & Carr Ltd for transfer pencils & paints; Geoffrey E. Macpherson Ltd for Madeira threads; Morris & Ingram for Badger airbrushes & textile paints; Offray Ribbons Ltd; Patons for wools & yarns; Tootal for threads; Whitecroft-Scovill Ltd for long bodkins and sewing requisites; Wilkinson Sword for embroidery and cutting-out scissors.

And finally, for their long-standing forbearance, those editors of B.T. Batsford Ltd who have been involved with this book.

# Introduction

Here is a book that is an absolute must for anyone contemplating quilting on the sewing machine. It is a straightforward and comprehensive guide, as useful to the beginner as to the skilled and experienced.

The mention of quilting conjures up to many people visions of patchwork bed-covers, but quilting is actually a sewing technique with many different three-dimensional forms. Basically, two layers of fabric are stitched together with a layer of filling sandwiched between. The stitching, which can be worked in a variety of patterns, holds the filling in place. The areas within the stitching puff up to produce a relief that can transform the surfaces of fabrics and textures, and adds an extra excitement to an otherwise flat piece of work, really bringing it to life.

The potential of the sewing machine has not yet been fully explored for its decorative, as well as its practical, applications. In this age of machines, the modern domestic sewing machine is surely one of the most versatile. It is immensely satisfying to use and enormous fun for quilting. Machine sewing is not a substitute for hand sewing – while both are creative skills they are entirely different operations. Machine sewing is precise, stronger and considerably faster.

The many and varied projects in this book represent only a tiny fraction of what can be achieved in machine quilting. Experimentation will be repaid a hundredfold. But remember also that while quilting is one of the most versatile of textile crafts, only practice and more practice will lead to perfection. Your machine will be your best friend, and like a best friend, it needs understanding and respect. You will experience immense enjoyment in the pursuit of machine quilting, as, indeed, have all the contributors to this book, not least the author herself!

# Design and Transferring the Design

There are sources of inspiration for three-dimensional quilting all around us, literally in every corner under the sun. However, an idea has to be recognized, and to adapt it to a new form it must be detached from the environment in which it was first observed. Carry a notebook in which to sketch or describe situations or objects, however simple, which appear to have potential, or use a camera to record ideas. Make notes about any special features, shadow effects or colour nuances which had particular appeal at the time.

A design to be stitched must demonstrate a perfect balance between the quilting method adopted, the textures and colours of the fabrics and thread, and the type of stitch employed. Moreover, the finished article must look – and be – in every way appropriate for the purpose for which it is intended.

The chapters which follow contain a wealth of ideas for design and pattern, but further source material can be found in:

- Museums and art galleries. Look for examples of textiles, quilts, embroideries, pottery, paintings, carvings, Art Deco, Art Nouveau, motifs on ancient artefacts, and old tiles.
- Libraries. Look at books about birds, animals, architecture, archaeology, design, stencilling, shells, nature study, biology, encyclopedias and children's books.
- The environment. Find inspiration in buildings, people, woodlands with leaves and trees, cloud effects, and fascinating wave patterns, the seaside with pebbles and shells, and the garden with birds, plants and insects.

1 The log pile – an inspiration for three-dimensional quilting. Anne Hulbert

Designs for the different aspects of quilting can be transferred to a large variety of fabrics in a number of ways, the most practical of which are given here. It is worth noting the following points.

Whichever method is used, do remember that the pattern usually has to be reversed when it is to be marked on the back of the work. It is most annoying to find the design the wrong way round on the front of the work.

The entire design should be planned and drawn out in full on paper. It is then ready to use as a working chart, and can later be stored flat for future use. Copies or tracings can be made of the design to cut up as separate templates of areas of the pattern.

Always test coloured markers and pencils on scrap fabric before use; and always read, and adhere to, manufacturers' instructions.

Much toil and trouble can be saved by keeping the number of lines to be transferred to the fabric to a minimum. Generally, only the main lines of a design need to be drawn out – it is not too difficult to quilt the rest by eye. However, do transfer these main lines on to the fabric before commencing any stitching – it is difficult to alter the design once the quilting is under way.

For corded quilting, with a single needle, it is only necessary to mark one of the pair of parallel lines. The distance to the second line is easily gauged by using the guide bar of the quilting foot. The side edge of the pressure foot also makes a reliable guide for stitching evenly spaced lines. With a double needle the distance from the first to the second line is, of course, already established by the gauge of the needle, whichever size is used.

**2** (top left) An arrangement of shells to develop for stuffed quilting. Use soft silk with a slight sheen, painted to resemble the shell markings. Anne Hulbert

**3** (top right) An old stone wall suggests ideas for quilted (wadded or stuffed) backgrounds, like the stencilled stonework in colour picture 19, 'Objets Trouvés'. The leaves of the winter heliotrope might be made separately (cutwork), and quilted and handstitched in place

## Materials and equipment for design

- Drawing and graph papers, plain and graph-ruled tracing paper, and carbon paper
- White card and thin white paper for making templates
- Pencils, rubber, ruler, drawing compass and drawing pins
- Masking tape, magitape and sellotape
- Pantograph for enlarging and reducing designs – these vary somewhat in design, so follow the maker's instructions.
- Access to a photocopying service – preferably one that has facilities for enlarging and reducing designs. Being quick and inexpensive, this is a useful service.

## Enlarging and reducing the design

**4** (below) Graph-ruled (1cm/1mm) tracing paper pinned over the original design to make the tracing

**5** (below right) The 'frame' marked round the traced design with the 1cm squares numbered

So often an inspiring illustration for a design is discovered in a book or magazine – or a sketch may have been made of a museum exhibit or a garden plant – but it is too large or too small. Should there be no copier or pantograph available for changing the size, the following technique is simple and satisfactory. For example, to enlarge a design to twice the size:

1. Pin or tape graph-ruled tracing paper (printed with 1cm/1mm squares) over the design and make a tracing of it as shown in Fig 4.

2. Draw a 'frame' round the traced design and number the 1cm squares along the top and down one side as shown in Fig 5.

3. On a separate sheet of graph tracing paper mark out a grid of 2cm squares – twice the size of the first – and number these as shown in Fig 6.

4. Carefully transfer the design on the 1cm grid to the 2cm grid, square by square, matching the pattern lines in the corresponding numbered squares, as shown in Fig 6.

For a different degree of enlargement, and for reductions, grids of proportionately larger or smaller measurements would be required. Should it be difficut to find graph tracing paper, plain tracing or thin white paper can easily be marked up into a grid, but accuracy is paramount.

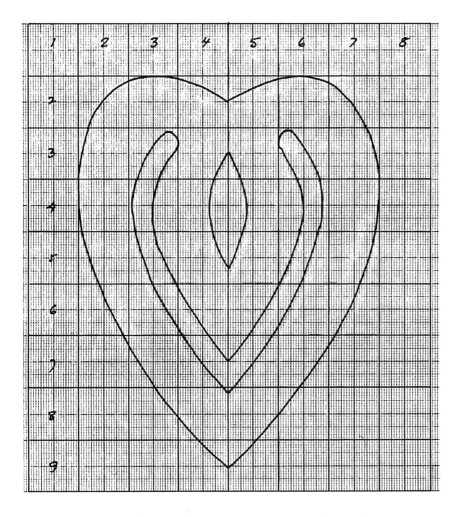

6 The grid enlarged to 2cm with the design marked out to match the corresponding squares of the 1cm grid (but now twice the size)

Designs for quilting may be applied to the front of the work (the right side of the fabric) or to the backing material at the back of the work. Generally, wherever possible, apply the pattern to the front, to make it easier to keep a close eye on the quality of the stitching and to check any movement of the fabric that might occur. However, for quilting dark, thick or heavily-textured fabrics, it is sometimes necessary to mark the backing and stitch the design from the back. This needs care, as the underside will be the front of the finished piece. The needle and bobbin tensions must be correct to result in perfect stitching on the front; and any movement of the fabric, with consequent puckering, must be avoided.

Iron the fabric to remove all creases before transferring the design – once quilted, it cannot be ironed again.

To achieve good clear lines and outlines, pin or tape the fabric, smooth and taut, to a firm surface. This makes the fabric easier to work on and more receptive for the design, whichever medium or method of application is used.

## Methods of transferring the design to the fabric

**Pencil**. This is one of the best types of marker to use on the right side of plain, light-coloured smooth fabrics, including delicate silks. Use a well-sharpened H or 2H – the fine lines, although faint, can be easily seen, will not smudge the fabric, and will last through the course of the work. The closeness of the machine stitches, providing the stitching is accurate, will conceal the light pencil markings, particularly if the lines are dotted, rather than solid and continuous. Light pencil markings will wash out, but never attempt to remove them with an india-rubber, which will only leave an irremoveable smudge.

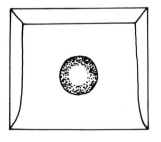

**7** Tailors' chalk in holder

**Tailors' chalk** (see Fig 7). Lines marked with this special chalk rub off easily, which can be a help (or a problem, if its marking is allowed to disappear before the work is done). It is best used on the wrong side, or on the backing fabric. However, it can be used on the right side of some fabrics, but first test to ensure that all traces will brush off. It will mark pale lines on dark fabrics, but must be kept well sharpened to a fine edge.

**Chalk pencils**. These have to be sharpened to a fine point to make a thin clear line on most fabrics. The marks can be erased with the brush attached to the end of the pencil, and they wash out quite well.

**Washable markers**. Called 'Wonder Markers', these can be washed out with plain water or a moistened cotton bud, after the design has been worked. Although the manufacturers recommend their use on the wrong side or on the backing, they can be used on the front of some natural materials. Again, test before use.

**Transfer pencils**. Available in light and dark colours, and best used for marking backing material, since the marks do not wash out of all natural fibres and not at all out of synthetics, particularly polyester. Draw or trace the design on tracing paper, then place it marked side down on the fabric to be quilted, and iron at moderate heat. This is a similar technique to that used for commercially-made embroidery transfers.

**Iron-on embroidery transfers**. Made of thin tissue paper, these have their patterns 'painted' in clear fine lines – dark for light colours and light for dark colours. These are particularly helpful to those who find difficulty in developing their own designs. A wide range of quilting patterns suitable for normal and free-motion stitching is available. They are best ironed on to the backing fabric as they are not guaranteed to wash out.

**Dressmakers' carbon paper**. Available in packets of light, dark and medium colours for marking different tones of fabric colour. As the carbon does not wash out, mark the wrong side or the backing. Place the carbon coloured side down on the backing fabric. Place the tracing of the design over the carbon paper with marked lines uppermost, so that they can be clearly seen. Now pin or tape both layers flat and taut, and work over the pattern with a sharp-pointed pencil or a tracing-wheel.

**Permanent markers**. Felt-tipped and strongly coloured. They will not wash out so are best used for marking the back, provided that the colour will not leak through to the front. However, they can be applied to the front for a bold project – their coloured lines can be used effectively as part of the design, and stitched and quilted.

**Direct tracing on to the fabric**. This is a very satisfactory method for marking either the face of the fabric at the front of the work, or the backing fabric behind. Most fine and semi-transparent fabrics can be used as a tracing medium. Draw the pattern with clear, dark lines on white paper. Lay the fabric right side up over the drawing, and pin both down securely, with the fabric smooth and taut. The design can then be traced directly on to the fabric.

**Window tracing**. This method is worth trying if the fabric is too opaque to see the design through it clearly. Place the fabric right side uppermost over the drawn pattern, and tape them together, against the light, on to a window pane. The design becomes clearly visible through the fabric and can now be traced on to it. If available, a photographic light-box will serve the same purpose – and with an easier working position, too.

**Tracing wheels** (see Figs 8a and 8b). These are rather like spurs, which were probably used originally and are made of metal or plastic. Lay paper tracing of the design over the fabric with the drawing facing upwards so as not to soil the fabric. Then run the serrated wheel over all the design lines in turn, leaving indented dotted lines on the fabric which should stay the course of the work. They could be joined up with a light pencil to last the duration of a large operation. Tracing wheels work well round card templates, and can be used on the front or back of any fabric that will show the wheel marks. They work well, also, in conjunction with dressmakers' carbon, leaving clear coloured dotted lines to stitch along.

**8a** Plastic tracing wheel

**8b** Metal tracing wheel used for marking the design through carbon paper

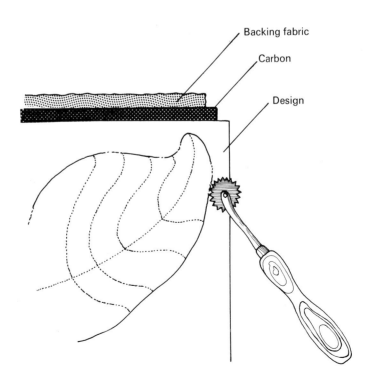

Backing fabric

Carbon

Design

**Marking round card templates**. This is a practical method of marking all-over and repeat patterns. Draw out the entire design on thin card and make a tracing to put aside as a working reference chart. Mark letters or numbers on the relative edges of each section where they are to match up again when drawn around on the fabric. Pin the fabric taut on to a firm surface. Cut the card into the shaped sections required for the pattern. Lay them in order on the pinned out fabric, matching all neighbouring letters or numbers, and lightly outline each with a suitable marker until the entire design has been marked.

**Stitching round paper templates**. In this instance the cut-out shapes, being paper, are more flexible. They can be tacked in place, to fit closely together on the fabric, but with just enough space to be able to stitch between each piece. The tacking stitches should be as near the edges of the templates as possible to prevent the machine turning them up during stitching. This method requires some practice and clearly works best with a few simple shapes and a design that is not too intricate.

**Commercially-printed fabrics**. Commercially-printed fabrics offer ready-made designs adaptable for all forms of quilting, especially useful for those who cannot draw. Not only can they be quilted on the right side for the front of the piece, they can also be tacked to the back and used as a pattern. In this case the design lines of the printed material are stitched on the wrong side, with the result that quite a different aspect of the original, without the printed colouring, appears on the front.

The practice of tacking tissue paper, with the design marked on it, to the fabric and stitching the design through it, is not really recommended. The tissue, being soft and lightweight, tends to get entangled in the feed-teeth, and it is almost impossible to extract all traces from the small close stitches of machine sewing.

## Applying design to fabrics by colouring

### Fabric colouring techniques

While all manner of manufactured printed fabrics have been quilted in the past (and still are) much imaginative and original work can now be created by colouring fabrics especially for quilting. This has become an important element in the art of quilting, every form of which can be successfully combined with any of a wide diversity of colouring techniques.

Many inspiring examples of machine quilting with dyed and painted backgrounds can be found throughout this book. They demonstrate how skilful colouring can greatly enhance the three-dimensional appeal of quilted work, and in some cases add an illusion of even greater depth between raised areas.

Study and experimentation are necessary to acquire the skill and there are several excellent books devoted to the subject. However, the following list suggests some of the interesting techniques involved in fabric colouring which are worth trying: Stencilling; spray-dyeing; batik; spatter painting; brush-painting; immersion dyeing; tie-dyeing; drawing with paint sticks; permanent marking.

Fabrics for colouring include natural materials like cotton, linen and silk, which are by far the most satisfactory. They absorb dye well, are easy to handle and always feel good. They ought to be washed before use to shrink them and to remove any dressing. Polyesters and some man-made fabrics tend to resist dyes – but nylon dyes quite well. There are, however, special dyes available for synthetics.

There is now a large and varied range of fabric colourants and dyes – Procion-M, Dylon Color-fun and Paint-Sticks, Caran D'Ache water soluble pencils, Deka, Rowney, Pentel, Badger and CarPlan spray-paints. They are readily available and easy to use, and between them they cater for most types of fabric. Manufacturers' instructions vary greatly; study them carefully.

**Further useful materials and equipment**
- Spare jars and small dishes for mixing paints
- Assorted paint brushes
- Cotton wool and cotton buds
- Blotting paper, kitchen paper and absorbent rags
- Stencil card or Manila (oiled) card
- Spray mount (but test for residual stickiness)
- Transparent self-stick film
- Stencil brushes, old toothbrushes, old shaving brushes
- Masking tape (but test for residual stickiness)
- Car and other spray-paints (preferably ozone-friendly)
- Airbrush and accessories

# Equipment for Machine Quilting

There are many makes of sewing machine and, although it is likely they will have different terms for the same attachments, their functions are common to most machines. Their uses and application will be fully illustrated and described in the handbook supplied by the manufacturer. Always keep the book to hand – it is an essential piece of equipment. If lost, the supplier of the machine can usually obtain a new one.

## Accessories for the machine

### Bobbin
This carries the underneath thread and is housed in a removable bobbin case. Keep plenty of spare bobbins, to avoid having to change over the type and colour of thread too frequently.

### Bobbin case
Keep several. The tension of the lower thread can, and should, be altered to suit the thickness of the thread used on the bobbin. It is easier to have two or three adjusted ready for use than suffer the irritation of repeatedly having to alter one. A tiny screw at the side of the case controls the flow of the thread. To tighten the tension for thinner threads, turn it clockwise; to loosen it, turn it anti-clockwise. But do not let it fall out.

**Presser feet**

The machine foot is clipped or screwed on and holds and helps to control the fabric during stitching. On most presser feet the centre is usefully marked by a groove – this is the point where the needle, when in its central position, penetrates the cloth. This is a great help, especially with appliqué and when satin stitching cut edges.

**Zig-zag foot** (the all-purpose foot). For zig-zag and double needle sewing. It has a wide hole to provide space for the needle to swing from side to side. It is generally used also for straight stitching.

**Quilting foot** – with quilting guide. On some machines the guide screws into the embroidery foot. The guide is an adjustable bar, used to keep rows of stitching straight and parallel.

**Embroidery foot**. A foreshortened foot for satin stitch and appliqué, double needle stitching and automatic patterns. It has a wider groove underneath, to allow the thickness of satin stitch and low corded channels to pass through without becoming flattened. Some models have a hole at the front, through which yarn is threaded and automatically taken under the stitches on the upper side of the fabric. It gives a padded effect to satin stitch, and a neat edge to cutwork. A thin cord or elastic thread may be used to gather material with the embroidery foot.

**Appliqué foot**. Made of transparent plastic, it gives a clear view of the edge of the motif as well as the stitching applying it to its ground material. The wide hole enables appliqué to be worked in zig-zag and satin stitches.

**Darning foot**. A round or rectangular enclosed shape offering close control of fabric movement and stitching. It enables the material to be moved about freely under the foot and is recommended for quilting with free-motion stitchery. When free-motion stitching is worked without an embroidery hoop, the presence of the darning foot provides some protection for the fingers.

**Braiding foot**. For couching. This has a large hole to the front, through which braid or yarn is threaded. It is then taken to the back under the foot and the needle, and automatically laid and stitched down (couched) on the upper side of the fabric with straight, zig-zag, satin or automatic stitching. On some machines the braiding foot has an adjustable notch for taking the braid through.

**Cording foot**. Similar to the braiding foot but has extra holes or grooves to accommodate up to five thin cords.

**Raised seam attachment**. Fitted over the needle plate, and used with a double needle. It is used for inserting a gimp thread into pin-tuck cording, on the underside of the material. Some machines have a hole in the needle plate through which the gimp can be threaded. It is this attachment that makes corded quilting on a single layer of fabric possible.

**Pin-tuck foot**. For use with double needles of different gauges. It is designed with grooves underneath to space up to nine parallel rows of pin-tucks.

**Zipper foot**. This is open on one side and resembles a half foot. The adjustable type is the best – it can be moved to the right or left, and allows stitching on both sides close against an edge that is higher on one side than the other.

**Further presser feet**. There are feet for making eyelets and for working circular embroidery, which can be attached to most modern machines. While both techniques may be used with most methods of quilting, they need considerable practice. Refer to the manufacturer's handbook and consult the retail supplier regarding the provision of these and numerous other accessories and presser feet.

### Feed-dog

This is the part under the needle plate holding the feed-teeth which, in normal sewing, grip the material and feed the work through the machine. But for free-motion stitching the teeth have to be covered or lowered, to allow the work to be moved freely in every direction. The handbook will advise whether or not a special plate is necessary to cover the moving feed-teeth. On machines not requiring a special plate, the feed-dog teeth can be lowered by simply turning a knob.

### Sewing machine needles

Sewing machine needles come in an assortment of sizes and have a variety of uses. It is always most important to use the correct make of needle for the particular make of machine. Of course, the size and type of needle must be right for the thread and the fabric with which it is to be worked. Never use blunt or bent needles: the former will snag the fabric and the latter could damage the machine. Check the state of the needle frequently and, when changing, make sure the new one is screwed very tightly into the needle clamp.

**Normal sewing needles**. For straight and zig-zag sewing. They are obtainable in European sizes ranging from 60 by tens up to 130 – the highest number being the thickest needle. The usual numbers for sewing are 80, 90 and 100, which are generally satisfactory for machine quilting. Heavier cloths and thicker threads will require thicker needles. American machine needles come in sizes 9, 11, 14, 16 and 18. Damage to fine and delicate materials can be avoided by using a fine needle, which will not make large holes. On the other hand, too small an eye can cause a sewing thread to split or break. If this happens, use a needle one size larger. For quilting in which several layers of materials are to be stitched use a 90 or 100 size needle.

**9** Double needles, sizes 1.5mm, 2mm, 3mm, 4mm, and a triple needle

**Ball-point needle**. This has a rounded point which makes it suitable for some knitted and synthetic fabrics, being less likely to cause damage to fibres.

**Leather needle**. This has a triangular or wedge-shaped point for stitching leather, vinyl and some plastic. The hole it makes closes itself, and is not left to gape.

**Double needle** (see Fig 9). This consists of a pair of needles fixed side by side to a single shank for insertion into the needle clamp. The space between the needles of course remains constant during stitching. Double needles are obtainable in gauges ranging from 1.6mm to 4.00mm. Two spools of thread are required for the top threading system. They interlock with a single bobbin thread, producing two parallel lines of stitches on the top, with the underneath stitching resembling zig-zag. A double needle can only be used in machines where the thread is normally passed through the needle from front to back, and not where it is threaded from side to side.

**Triple needle** (see Fig 9). Similar to a double needle but having three needles attached to a single shank.

Always keep a good supply of machine needles in different sizes. Waddings and filling materials are not kind to them, and is surprising how quickly they pass their best. Always discard a doubtful needle.

## Sewing machine oil and cleaning brush

With machine quilting, fluff from the filling materials soon collects under the needle plate and quickly builds up. Brush it out frequently, since otherwise the caked fluff will cause broken threads, bent needles and tension problems.

When used frequently for quilting, the machine will need oiling more than for normal sewing. Use a brand recommended by the manufacturer of the machine and apply it at the end of the day. Then run the machine for a minute or two, and leave overnight for the oil to settle. Before using again, wipe off any excess oil with a tissue.

## Embroidery ring or hoop (see Fig 10)

This has its 'pros and cons'. It will certainly hold the work taut during stitching, which is helpful. Also, because it is usually held at the sides,

**10** The embroidery hoop being used for free-motion stitching on wadded fabrics

it keeps the fingers away from the needle, and therefore offers some protection – an important consideration with free-motion stitching. However, an embroidery hoop is inclined to leave a ring mark on the work which cannot always be eradicated, since quilted materials cannot be ironed properly. Moreover, except for small projects, the maximum size available (see below) is rather limited for machine quilting, making it necessary to change its position frequently. A wooden hoop will grip fabric better than one made of metal, but it must be very smooth indeed. The inner ring should be bound with tape to prevent the fabric slipping during stitching.

Place the hoop in the machine for stitching with the wrong side of the work facing downwards, absolutely flat on the machine bed – the right side faces upwards from inside the hoop. However, as in cable stitch, when a thick thread is wound on the bobbin, the right side then faces downwards. Should it be difficult to fit the hoop into position, lower the feed-dog, remove the presser foot (and the needle also, if necessary), slide the hoop into position and replace the foot and needle. Embroidery rings are available in sizes up to 30cm (12in) diameter. Machine retailers sell special small steel hoops between 5cm (2in) and 12cm (5in) diameter.

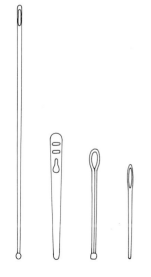

11 Cording 'needles'. From left; long (150mm/ 6in) ball-point threader, flat bodkin, 'split' bodkin, blunt-ended needle

## General sewing requisites

- Scissors – large sharp ones for cutting out, and a small pair of embroidery scissors with narrow blades and sharp points for intricate work
- Tape measure
- Long and short steel pins
- Needles for handsewing
- Seam-ripper

**Extras required for corded quilting** (see Fig 11).
A cording 'needle' is required for drawing the yarn filling through the stitched channels. There are numerous styles and sizes of bodkins and tapestry needles available with a large eye and a blunt or rounded end for doing this. Do not use a sharp pointed tool – it might pierce the materials and leave unsightly holes in the work.

## Extras required for stuffed quilting

A stuffing stick is required for pushing the filling into the stitched pockets. Suitable 'sticks' are: wooden skewers of different sizes, obtainable from the butcher; cuticle sticks from the chemist; or a pencil with a broken point. Again, do not use anything with a sharp point.

Wadded, flat and shadow quilting, and padded work do not require any special tools or equipment further to those mentioned above.

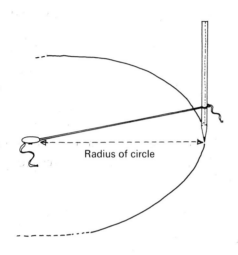

Radius of circle

12 A useful 'compass' for drawing circles larger than the normal compass can manage. It is simple to make: (a) cut a notch round a pencil, about 25mm (1in) from the point, and tie one end of a length of string tightly round it. (b) Push a drawing pin through the string at the measured distance from the pencil – this will be the radius of the circle required. (c) Press the pin firmly into paper, and work surface. (d) Draw the circle, keeping the string taut and the pencil vertical all the time. Do not dismantle the compass – keep it for future use

# Fabrics and Fillings

There can really be no hard and fast rules for choosing fabrics for quilting on the sewing machine. Although they behave differently and have different functions, most types of material can be quilted by one method or another, just so long as the machine has the ability to cope.

When it comes to choosing from a boundless variety of colours, textures and weights, the outcome of the finished piece is paramount. Is it to be decorative or purely functional, or a combination of both – and, just as important, where is it going to end up? Bear the following in mind:

- When the quilting is planned for garments and household articles, the materials for the top, the backing and the lining have to be washable (or at least dry-cleanable), pre-shrunk and colourfast. If there is any doubt, test-wash sample pieces before embarking on a project – afterwards will be too late.
- Soft, stretchy materials like jersey and other knitted fabrics are easy to mould, and can produce a very soft, comfortable relief, particularly with stuffed quilting. However, being so pliable, they are not always the easiest to sew by machine, so a special presser-foot and/or a ball-point needle will help.

It is important to get accustomed to handling different fabrics. Feeling their textures and weights is as essential as studying their appearances. Try wrapping material round a closed fist and twisting and turning it to see the effects of light from different angles. Or arrange it in folds and hold it up to the light. Take into account, too, the colour relationships between plain and printed fabrics.

It is a good idea to build up a bank of fabric samples to use for trying out quilting methods. Worked examples can be kept as references for futher use, particularly if details of the techniques tried out are noted on the back with a permanent marker. Inexpensive short lengths of fabric remnants can always be found at remnant counters and at end-of-line stores.

## Top fabrics

The main factor in choosing a top fabric (for the front of the work) is its appearance – always on show, its colour and texture must look good. There is a wide and wonderful range of colours, from the very palest to the most vivid and vibrant, to choose from. As for texture, the variety is probably even greater – from the finest, softest voiles and silks, through to heavy linens, velvets, knobbly tweeds and rough hessian.

Suppleness is also important: the top material must have some 'give' in order to create a raised design. It should be more supple than the backing, in order to throw the padded areas forward to the front. Too hard a top fabric will result in a well quilted backing!

Natural woven materials like cotton, silk and wool are reasonably 'giving' and quilt better than their woven synthetic counterparts – they are less hard and springy, more versatile and generally easier to handle. Even so, synthetic knitted fabrics, including jersey and stretch velvet, quilt excellently, with well-moulded three-dimensional results. Soft chamois leathers, kid and suedes, being naturally pliable, can, depending on their thickness, be used most successfully for most methods of machine quilting.

Always consider, too, whether or not the material is well suited to the design and the method of quilting. Heavily textured, loosely-woven material, for instance, would not make a satisfactory top surface for corded or stuffed quilting. It would be difficult to achieve neat edges to raised shapes and linear patterns, and the fillings would show through.

Plain colours show off a quilted design best of all. Silk, glazed chintz and soft velvet particularly catch the light on raised areas, thus creating a marked contrast with the shadows made by stitching into and around a padded design.

Printed fabrics may be used providing their patterns do not compete with, or detract from, a good quilted design. Some materials with ready-made designs could, in some situations, benefit from quilting: striped patterns call for corded quilting, while sectioned designs lend themselves well to stuffed quilting. Several examples of quilting on printed fabric are shown in this book.


## Filling materials

It is of course the filling which moulds and holds the shape of the relief work. The choice of filling materials for any form of quilting must be entirely governed by the purpose of the finished article. For example, garments will, in the main, require a soft, light and washable wadding or cord filling, whereas floor coverings need firm, hardwearing padding.

**Fillings suitable for wadded quilting**

**Synthetic wadding** (bonded polyester or Terylene (Dacron) fibre with a fire-resistant finish). The best known and most popular filling. It is usually white and comes in sheet form 'off the roll'. Different thicknesses and widths (90cm (36in) to 200cm (80in)) are available and sold by ounce weight per square yard – 2 oz, 4 oz, etc, up to 10 oz, and 14 oz. A good quality brand of man-made wadding is light and easy to use, and, being springy, quilts beautifully. Nevertheless, the thicker the layer of wadding the more likely it is to pucker when quilted. Should joining be necessary, hand-sew the edges loosely together with a large herring-bone stitch. Polyester wadding is inexpensive, safe, clean and washable. Do not use unbonded synthetic wadding – its fibres can work through the top fabric and be visible on the front of the work.

**Domette**. A cream-coloured loosely-knitted, fluffy cotton material that produces a low-level quilting.

**Plastic foam**. A fairly dense material but very good for quilting stool tops and chair seats and backs, where a firm, hardwearing and cleanable padding is required. Be certain to use only a safe, fireproof variety. Foam is sold by the 'piece' in a wide range of thicknesses. It is not wise to quilt foam without a backing as it can stick to the needle plate during stitching.

**Wool, felt, flannel, terry-towelling and blanket material**. All good heat insulators, these may also be used as fillings, but although very warm, they are on the heavy side and the quilting will be rather flat. Being likely to shrink (hence necessitating dry-cleaning) they are best used to pad floor rugs, wall-hangings and artwork.

**Cotton batting**. This too is on the heavy side. It has a tendency to go lumpy and shift out of place when washed.

Some (fortunately few) sewing machines allow little room between the presser foot and the feed-dog, so that thickly wadded quilting cannot easily be taken through. Check the situation before starting work in order to avoid later frustration and potential disappointment.

### Fillings suitable for corded quilting

In corded quilting the filling must be a strand of some sort of material which is threaded through the space between lines of stitching. It is therefore of the greatest importance that the quilting yarns properly fit the channels in which they are to be inserted. All the channels must finish up well-raised and evenly filled with the correct thickness of yarn, whatever the width of the channels and the type of filling. Too thick a filling is difficult to draw through, and will stretch the fabric and pull the stitches out of alignment. Too thin a yarn shifts within the channel, leaving uneven thinly-padded areas. A hard rough cord is capable of wearing out the fabric.

**Quilting wool**. Very soft and pure, but shrinkable and sold in rather expensive hanks. Its main advantage is its lack of 'twist' – it has no ridges to make the finer fabrics look lumpy. It is good for corded quilting on delicate silks that can be dry-cleaned.

**Knitting yarns** (the man-made variety). These are soft and lightweight, with low twist levels, and no washing problems.

**Cotton and rayon crochet yarns**. These are plentiful and inexpensive. They come in a wide range of colour and thickness, and are straightforward to insert by hand, or automatically by some machines.

**Piping cords, parcel strings, garden twines and macramé cords**. These all seem rather hard and bulky, but inserted into large wide channels they are fun to use in artwork – hangings, screens and even pelmets.

**Novelty 'cording'**. Narrow strips of materials, strings of beads and grasses are fun to use for filling the channels on special projects.

To estimate the length of yarn required for filling the channels in a design, measure the total length of stitched channels to be padded, and allow a little extra for 'take-up' and for the loops and ends to be left at curves and corners.

Insertion cords should, as far as possible, be washed before use in case they shrink or their colours rub off or run– even if their labels state otherwise!

### Fillings suitable for stuffed quilting

In stuffed quilting, where areas of a design are raised individually, it is most important that the end result is not just a collection of hard and lumpy motifs. A soft, lightweight washable filling material is ideal.

**Polyester toy-filling**. Provided it conforms to safety standards, this is one of the best for general work. It is safe, washable, does not shrink or stretch, and dries quickly. It is also very resilient, unlikely to lose its shape when washed, and easy and pleasant to work with. It should be a well-carded quality to give a high bulk/weight ratio with a soft but springy touch.

**Kapok**. This is often used, but can be trying to work with, since the fibres can irritate the eyes and nose. Moreover, it is heavy and difficult to mould evenly and can shrink when washed.

**Chopped foam** (the safe kind) can be used for some projects using heavily-textured materials. But it would be rather lumpy for lightweight fabrics.

**Wool**. Although moths love it, wool can provide warmth where large areas are stuffed. However, it is likely to shrink when washed, spoiling the shapes in the design.

**Left-over scraps and off-cuts of polyester sheet wadding** are well worth keeping, however small, for padding individual shapes. Tease them out well, chop them up and use as for toy-filling.

*Note*: Cotton and cotton wool are not recommended. They feel heavy and are too easily packed into hard lumps. When washed they shrink, and lose shape.

## Fillings suitable for shadow quilting

As well as the traditional low-level method, shadow quilting may be combined with wadded, corded and stuffed quilting. And, provided the top fabric is transparent, there is an infinite assortment of colourful and highly-textured filling materials that can be used for any of those methods.

In wadded shadow-work, it is better to use low-fraying fillings – for example, felt, leather, plastic, painted Vilene, printed fabrics and tinsel paper.

For filling stitched channels on a transparent fabric, try tapisserie wools, knitting yarns, threaded beads, strips of printed cloth, and leather and plastic thonging.

Unusual and exciting effects can be achieved by filling stitched pockets in stuffed quilting with chopped fabrics and wools, or glittery beads and sequins, or even hair, shells, dried flowers, seeds and grain.

There are many exotic and seemingly unlikely fillings to try and it is worth spending time experimenting with them behind different see-through materials – the dramatic effects can be especially good for wall-hangings and other artwork.


# Backing fabrics

Almost all methods of quilting need a backing to hold the padding or other raising material in place. The top and backing fabrics are stitched together whether a padding is sandwiched between them before stitching, or inserted from the back after the stitching.

To ensure that the highest contours appear on the front of the work, the backing material used for all quilting methods needs to be firmer than the top fabric and must have no 'stretch'. When the front and backing fabrics are of similar weights the height of the raised areas will also be similar, producing an equally quilted back (Fig 13). There are plenty of good inexpensive cloths for backing, including calico in different weights, organza, cotton and poly-cotton, chintz and muslin (but not 'butter' muslin, which is too loose and limp). Heavy fabrics can be used to back heavy pictures and hangings, as long as the machine can manage to stitch throughout the layers.

Quilting on circular articles like round cushions can be trouble-some, and result in puckering and a distorted outline. This can be guarded against if the front and backing materials are joined with the

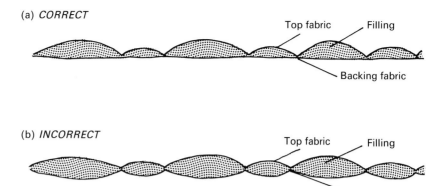

13 (a) Correct quilting with a firmer backing than top fabric, producing a well-raised design on the right side. (b) Incorrect quilting with a backing that is too lightweight for the top, producing an equally raised design on each side

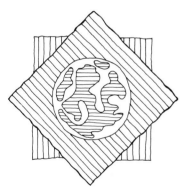

14 A deterrent against distortion and puckering when quilting circular articles. The front and backing fabrics are layered with the grain of one diagonally across the other

grain of one running across the other – the two layers prevent each other from stretching out of shape (see Fig 14).

Printed fabrics, when used to back quilting, can at the same time take the place of a marked-out design, and be worked from the back. The stitched outline of the design then appearing on the front can be very attractive, without the actual colouring of the print showing.

If the backing material is likely to be seen, it should match, or tone with, the colour of the front. Otherwise a white or cream-coloured material is generally suitable.

Any fabric intended for the backing must be washed before use, as a safeguard against subsequent shrinking and colour bleeding.

## Lining fabrics

If the back of the work on a finished quilted piece is likely to be seen, then it must be lined, or covered over, to conceal pattern lines, the wrong side of the stitching and thread ends.

To look neat and professional, the lining must be compatible with the front of the work in colour, texture and weight, so that the completed article looks good from all angles. However, where the lining will be hidden within a finished article, matching it to the front is not so crucial.

It is also sensible to line the back of corded and stuffed quilting, particularly when the filling has been inserted through holes made in the backing fabric. Lining will protect these weak spots against wear and tear. Quilted cushions will last longer if this principle is followed.

Lining fabric should not be heavy or coarse-textured – it is only to be used as a covering. It can be cut from left-over scraps if they are large enough; otherwise use muslin, cotton lawn, curtain lining or similar lightweight fabrics.

Cut the lining piece to the same size as the back of the quilted article. Then tack it in place all round the sides, through all layers of materials, and include in the seams when making up the article.

## Bonding fabrics

These help a great deal in appliqué work, and when making free-standing motifs, to prevent fraying of edges. Bondaweb, Bondina and the iron-on Vilene products are easy to use and washable, and they can be cut to any shape. They are available from haberdashery counters and fabric departments.

When buying fabrics for machine quilting, make allowances for the 'take-up' caused by the quilting. Buy extra, also, to allow for mistakes, matching patterns on prints, and for making something else in the same material.

Again it must be stressed – always test wash new fabrics to be used for the top, backing, and lining for shrinkage and colour bleeding.

# Threads and Stitching

## Threads for machine quilting

The choice of thread for machine quilting is greatly influenced by the quilting method, the purpose of the work and the nature of the fabric. In addition to the excellent traditional types made for machine sewing, there is available an outstanding array of interesting and luxurious threads, such as metallic, silk, cotton and rayon. Quilting can often be much improved by substituting a novel thread, rich in colour and texture, for a plain dull one. But there are undoubtedly plenty of times when it is appropriate to use the more ordinary threads.

When a thread is too thick or bulky to be passed through the needle it can be wound on to the bobbin, by the machine method or by hand, and stitched from the underside. Very thick threads and yarns can be couched on to the fabric from the top. On wadded quilting the laid yarn then sinks into the padded layers of materials and can look very attractive.

To achieve the best results, test sewing threads as far as possible for performance and effect and also for shrinkage and bleeding.

Never use cheap thread. It splits and breaks all too easily, so will not last long in the work, and can tangle in the machine. Also, it is likely to shrink and the colour to bleed.

### Tacking (basting) threads

Do not use too thick a thread for tacking, as it might leave holes and long indentations in padded materials. Otherwise end-of-reel oddments of thread can be used up for tacking. The colour of the thread should differ markedly both from that of the top material and of the quilting threads to be used. This will assist easy identification when it comes to removing them. Special tacking thread can be bought inexpensively in larger spools and very large cones.

### Cotton threads

One hundred per cent cotton and mercerized cotton are supplied in a great variety of colours. Various thicknesses are made, and are gauged by numbers – the higher the number the thinner the thread. Number 30, being quite coarse, is for heavy duty work, while number 60, which is very fine, is for delicate quilting. It is easier and more economical to use these for the bobbin when novelty threads are to be used for the top system.

### Polyester threads

Made of one hundred percent polyester, these have become the everyday, all-purpose machine threads that withstand hot washing and hot ironing, and are fadeless. They are strong, yet 'give' well with the fabric and, when used for machine quilting, their elasticity helps to prevent the stitching from puckering quilted layers of materials.

### Pure silk

Silk stitches well and always looks correct on silk materials. It has good elasticity and is suitable for quilting many fabrics. Silk thread is obtainable on spools for machine sewing in a very wide range of colours. Some makes are washable, others have to be dry-cleaned.

### Rayon

This has a beautiful sheen, and catches the light like silk. It comes in a wide range of plain and variegated colours and looks very good worked on the front of an article. Useful for straight and satin stitch, and automatic patterns, rayon comes in different weights. Should the thread snap, change to a larger needle.

Rayon thread can slip down its spool, wind itself round the spool holder and break. Certain machines have a special accessory to prevent this happening. But if not, the situation can be simply avoided by taping a tapestry needle, eye upwards, about 50cm (2in) to the left of the spool holder on the machine (see Fig 15).

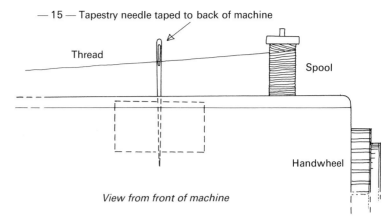

— 15 — Tapestry needle taped to back of machine

Thread

Spool

Handwheel

*View from front of machine*

**15** A tapestry needle in use as an extra thread guide. It will hold the thread high and prevent it from winding and tangling itself round the spool holder

On the bobbin, use a normal thread in a matching colour: rayon is rather slippery, and it would also be wasteful to use on the wrong side where it will not show.

## Machine embroidery threads

There are a number of wonderful plain, coloured and variegated embroidery threads for machine stitching. As a rule they are finely-textured with a sheen that gives a lustrous appearance to close satin stitch. Their softness and flexibility makes them especially suitable for free-motion stitching on lightweight fabrics.

## Metallic threads

There is available an exciting collection of decorative metallic threads – gold, silver, copper, variegated, lurex, and many more. Generally they are washable and dry-cleanable. There are finely-textured threads for quilting from the top, and bulkier, coarsely-textured threads that are best stitched from the underside of the work. Straight, zig-zag, satin and automatic pattern stitching with metallic thread can enrich a piece of quilting significantly. The thinner qualities can be used successfully for free-motion stitching through padded layers of materials. And stitching parallel lines for corded quilting in metallic threads can often be more interesting than if a plain thread were used.

## Invisible (transparent) nylon threads

Although this is pretty tough and inclined to be rather stiff, it can be used quite effectively for the top, with a coloured thread on the bobbin. It can also be used to couch braids and thick yarns when a

35

solid colour of thread is not required. However, some types are rather hard; they might leave holes and can tear fabric, and hence could outlive the article being made.

There are many more threads suitable for quilting on the sewing machine. Some are sold in hanks and can be wound on to a spool for top sewing, or on to the bobbin for sewing from underneath. They can be bought from specialist needlework shops, department stores and fabric shops. Search them out and try them out!

## Tacking (basting) for quilting

The main problem for the machine quilter is puckering. This can happen when two or more thicknesses of fabric shift relative to each other during stitching. The needle and thread have to penetrate all the layers many times in order to quilt. With every stitch the work is jerked forward, so it is no wonder that the layers tend to slip out of alignment. Do not despair – the basis of all well turned out work is good preparation, and the secret is proper tacking (basting) to hold all layers firmly together. Although some machines are capable of tacking, it can be done more thoroughly by hand. Keep the following general points in mind when tackling this very important stage of all machine quilting:

- Use a long, fine needle to avoid holes being left in the fabric.
- Take the needle vertically in and out of the materials – slanting the needle could cause the layers to move sideways.
- Tack, wherever possible, from the right side of the work, making only small tacking stitches on the underside – they are less likely to catch in the feed-dog teeth of the machine. Make longer stitches on the top.
- Start at the centre and tack outwards to the corners and sides, smoothing the materials towards them.

There is no need to re-start at the centre each time with a new thread if a long end is left at the start of the first line, and not pulled through. Thread the needle with this long end and tack in the opposite direction (see Fig 16). This is a time-saver.

- Pull the thread, firmly but gently, to draw the layers together so they cannot shift about – in fact, the tacking will look like quilting.

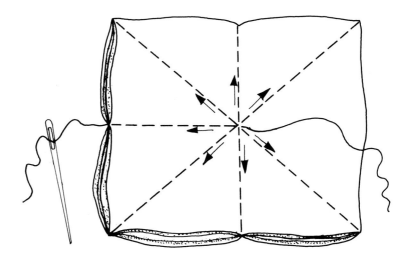

**16** Tacking layers of materials together from the centre outwards

- Do not skimp on the tacking. Tack plenty of good straight lines about 75mm (3in) apart to ensure well-secured layers of materials ready for stitching.
- Never iron the work after tacking – if the stitches are ironed their marks will remain.

## Stitching to quilt

The modern 'swing-needle' sewing machines have the ability to produce zig-zag, satin and automatic fancy stitching, and will take a double or treble needle. These facilities provide almost limitless potential for machine quilting.

Older machines, although restricted to sewing in a simple straight (running) stitch, nevertheless have the ability to produce very beautiful quilted articles, and can cope with most of the threads discussed earlier.

The majority of machine stitching techniques can be used for sewing designs on the different forms of machine quilting, whether one or several layers of material are to be used. There are some superb combinations to be explored.

Before commencing any stitching:

- Check the top tension and increase or decrease it as necessary to suit the spool thread. Do the same with the bobbin to suit the lower thread.

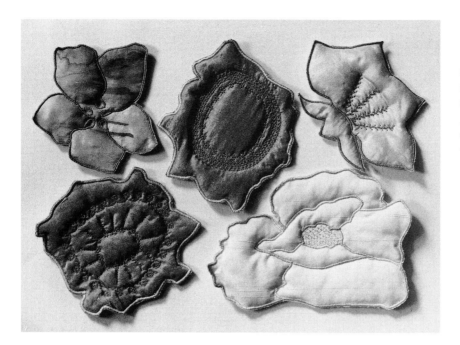

**17** Padded motifs showing a variety of stitching techniques, including cutwork, eyelet stitching, and pretty automatic patterns. Fine gold metallic, silk, rayon and cotton threads were used. Anna Donovan

- Adjust settings for stitch width and stitch length as required for straight stitch or zig-zag.
- Adjust the pressure of the presser foot on the materials to suit their thickness (on some machines this is done automatically and cannot be altered).
- Try the stitching on oddments of the materials to be used for the actual quilting, and keep a note of all settings for later reference.
- Make sure there is sufficient thread of the correct type and colour to complete the stitching.
- Always begin the quilting at the centre of the design and work outwards, first one way and then in the opposite direction.
- Allow the machine to take the work through – on no account help it. Even the slightest pushing or pulling might cause puckering, and even breakage of the needle.
- Support the fabrics on the left of the needle plate with your left hand to prevent it from slipping sideways. Guide the work lightly with your right hand.
- Linear patterns must be stitched in straight, even lines. The needle plate is marked with guidelines 3mm ($\frac{1}{8}$in) apart, against which the fabric edge can be aligned. The edge of the presser foot also makes a useful guide. The quilting bar will aid the

stitching of uniformly-spaced parallel lines. For stitching lines even wider apart than the guides suggested above can manage, stick masking tape to the machine bed at the required distance, and align the edge of the material to the edge of the tape.

- The stitching must be accurate throughout the work to make certain the pattern markings are entirely concealed, particularly if they are on the front. Guide the pattern line under the central notch on the front of the presser foot as the work is taken through the machine.
- Stitch lines as long and continuous as possible to avoid over-frequent and inconvenient stopping and starting, and also to reduce the number of thread ends to be tied off.
- Do not stitch in reverse to start the sewing, or end it off – this would leave an untidy mass of stitches showing on the front. Take all ends of thread through to the back and darn them into the material; or tie them in pairs and cut to leave ends about 12mm ($\frac{1}{2}$in) from the knot.
- Mistakes are best not made – machine stitches, being small and interlocked, are very difficult to unpick, and they leave holes in the work.

Stitchery for machine quilting need not be limited to straight running stitches. Zig-zag and satin stitching (closed-up zig-zag), and automatic pattern stitching, can produce delightful alternatives. There is a real wealth of opportunity. Imagine the effect of different stitches on wadded quilting; try fancy stitching round motifs for stuffed quilting; and linear patterns for corded quilting.

### Zig-zag and satin stitching

Zig-zag and satin stitches are controlled by the stitch-width and stitch-length knobs. The former sets the width of the stitching from zero (running stitch), up to 4 or 5 to form zig-zag and satin stitching, with a width of about 4mm ($\frac{3}{16}$in). The stitch-length knob controls the spacing of the stitches – the nearer to '0' it is set, the closer together the stitches become to form satin stitch. Experiment on a range of fabrics using various combinations of stitch settings and threads – many interesting patterns can be developed. Close zig-zag and satin stitching requires a slightly looser top tension than normal sewing to prevent the bobbin thread being seen on the front. Puckering of the fabric by the close satin stitching also indicates loosening of the top tension.

## Automatic pattern stitching

Automatic decorative patterns are now an integral feature of the modern machine. The patterns, which include circular and eyelet embroidery, vary from machine to machine, are very decorative and can mostly be incorporated into wonderful ideas for quilting. They are very effective as textural backgrounds to the raised areas of stuffed quilting, and also between the channels of corded quilting. Although the designs are very regular they can, like zig-zag stitching, be varied greatly by combining the different stitch width and length settings with different threads.

## Free-motion stitching

This is a fast and impressive way of stitching small and intricate patterns for quilting, since the fabric can be steered freely in any direction– to the left, to the right, forward and backward, and in circles. After lowering or covering the feed-teeth, 'trace' the design around with the machine needle from the front or the back. The technique needs practice but, once mastered, it offers more freedom and greater manoeuvrability in stitching, as well as being great fun and immensely satisfying. With free-motion stitching it is possible to travel long distances without accumulating a number of thread ends which either require fastening off, or may become entangled in the machine.

An embroidery hoop may be used for free-stitching patterns for stuffed and flat quilting, but with wadded quilting there may be too much thickness to fit into the ring. In this case, the layers of materials will provide a firm base for the sewing, and fitting a darning foot will protect the fingers. The flat-bed extension should be fitted for free-motion stitching to prevent the work, whether in a hoop or not, from tipping over the edge. Always start with the bobbin thread drawn through to the top so that it cannot tangle underneath. Work a few stitches and cut the threads close to the fabric – they are unlikely to come undone. Always keep the presser bar lowered to retain the top tension. Stitch size is determined by the movement of the work: the slower it is steered about, the smaller the stitch; the faster it is moved, the larger the stitch. On no account force the work in any direction. This could break the thread, and also the needle, which might in turn then damage the needle plate.

It is also well worth trying out zig-zag and satin stitches and decorative patterns in free-motion stitching on designs for different methods of machine quilting – there is much to discover from mixing methods and materials.

## Couching

Couching is a technique in which a thick thread or yarn is laid on to the background and stitched down by a finer thread. It is used to apply materials too heavy and thick for the needle threading system. Any material the needle will penetrate (or 'reach over' as in zig-zag) can be couched. Highly decorative bulky yarns, novel braids, wire and dried grasses can be couched to flat and wadded surfaces of fabrics by machine, with straight stitch down the middle of the 'braid', or with zig-zag across its width. Automatic patterns can also be used (see Fig 18). Interesting textural backgrounds for raised corded and stuffed designs can derive from closely, or attractively scattered,

**18** A variety of bulky materials couched on to different wadded surfaces. Top section, on white silk: rayon ric-rac braid, metallic gold wrapping 'string', millinery wire, metallic silver tape, velvet rouleau and twisted cord. Centre section, on heavy 'trellis' patterned furnishing cotton: thick knitting yarns couched with running, zig-zag, satin and automatic stitches. Bottom section, on calico: lampshade braid, rug wool, satin ribbon and lacing

couched threads. And outlines of shapes in wadded quilting can be greatly emphasized by the extra detail of a couched thread, almost adding another dimension to the quilting.

The braiding foot, the cording foot, the embroidery foot and the buttonhole foot can all be used for couching. These have a groove underneath, through which to guide the thread being couched. Should they not be available use a general purpose foot. The procedure is to lay the yarn on the fabric and fasten it down with pins at right angles across it. Keeping the yarn held fairly taut and centred to the notch at the front of the foot, stitch along it, removing the pins as they are approached.

## Cable stitching

A bold decorative stitch, cable stitch resembles couching, but is worked with a thick thread on the bobbin, and with the right side of the work facing downwards. Wind cotton perle (pearl), crochet cotton or a metallic thread on the bobbin, and decrease the tension sufficiently for it to run easily. Thread the top system with a normal thread or, alternatively, a fine metallic or silk thread. Increase the top tension to draw the bobbin thread into the fabric, thus creating the 'cable' effect on the right side with the thicker thread. Unlike ordinary stitching, the bobbin thread is too thick to be pulled right through the fabric by the top thread. Always bring the bobbin thread through to the top before beginning to stitch, and at the end of stitching, and finish by hand. Cable stitch may be worked with an exciting variety of threads on the bobbin, adding richly textured effects to wadded quilting.

## Using metallic threads

Metallic threads can give a wonderfully luxurious look to wadded quilting. There are numerous metallic threads fine enough to be taken through the top system, and threaded through the eye of the needle. They can also be used with double and triple needles for stitching on the front; and for free-motion stitchery too. A size 90/100 needle suits most thin metallic threads, but if the thread splits, change it for a larger size, say 100/110. The top tension is best loosened a little to prevent the bobbin thread from being drawn up to show on the front. Zig-zag, satin and automatic stitches may also be worked in metallic threads, again with a slacker top tension. Use an ordinary polyester or cotton thread, in a matching colour, for the bobbin. The speed of the machine should be slower than normal.

Bulkier metallic threads, too thick for the needle eye, can be wound on the bobbin. In this case, mark and stitch the design on the back of the work, which faces upwards (the front, with the metallic thread, faces downwards).

### Double needle stitching

The double needle stitches uniform pairs of parallel lines on the front, while the back resembles zig-zag stitch, so the fabric is not reversible. It can produce corded quilting quickly on a single layer of fabric as well as adding innovative decoration to other forms of quilting.

Zig-zag stitching and automatic patterns can be worked with a double needle, but be cautious when varying the stitch width and length – do not allow the needle to swing against the needle plate. Refer to the manufacturer's handbook for threading instructions, and if possible pass one thread each side of the tension disc to reduce the likelihood of them twisting together during stitching.

Threading each of the pair of needles with a thread of a different colour or texture – for instance, bright metallic in one and silk in the other – will lead to decorative rainbow effects. Then try using them to stitch wavy lines over a large plain area, or over the background of a more intricate design.

With the two needles together, corners cannot be turned as simply as with a single needle. Proceed as follows: Lower the points of the needles just into the fabric. Lift the presser foot. Half turn the fabric and then lower the presser foot. Turn the handwheel (by hand) to make one stitch, leaving the needle points in the fabric. Lift the presser foot and complete the turn. Finally, lower the presser foot and continue the stitching.

Double needle stitching is not the easiest of techniques for small areas of detailed pattern, because the needles are awkward to manoeuvre in confined spaces. But they are an important type of needle to keep for quick corded quilting over large areas in straight or random wavy lines, on their own, or incorporated in the other methods of quilting.

### Pleating and tucking

Though not a stitching method, using pleated fabrics can add yet a further dimension to quilting as shown in the 'Duck On Lily Pond' photograph (see Fig 36). There are other ways of quilting pleated material, one of which is as follows (see Fig 19):

- Stitch rows of pleats across the top fabric.
- Tack together the pleated fabric, a layer of wadding and the backing.
- Stitch across the pleats, through all layers – at right angles to them – so they all face in the same direction.
- Stitch back across the pleats to make them all face in the opposite direction.
- Stitch a third row similar to the first.

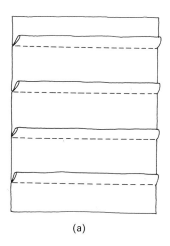

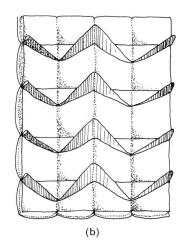

(a)  (b)

**19** Stitching across a pleated surface in different directions to create further dimensions to a fabric, prior to quilting it.
(a) The pleated single layer of fabric. (b) The pleated fabric quilted – the pleats are twisted by lines of stitching running in opposite directions, presenting further texture and dimension

A variety of patterns on the wadded pleating can emerge by (a) varying the width of the pleats; (b) varying the spacing of stitching lines across the pleats; (c) using different stitches; (d) using a double needle; and (e) cord-quilting the rows of stitching. Quilting pleated silks and satins gives them a very rich appearance indeed.

Further details of specialized stitching techniques will be found in the relevant chapters on the different forms of machine quilting which follow.

# Wadded Quilting

20 Victorian tile. An old pattern to work with free-motion stitching on padded materials

An age-old form of quilting, the wadded technique was originally used more than any other for warmth and comfort combined with softness, in the making of garments, footwear, bedding and floor coverings. Hand-sewn, the work was always laborious and time-consuming. Today, the sewing machine can quickly stitch patterns over wadded materials to create any number of useful and beautiful articles. The depth of the quilting into the layers of fabrics and wadding causes shadows, making a pleasing contrast between the raised lighter areas and the sunken stitched lines. Using a darker thread gives the illusion of greater depth.

The principle of wadded quilting is straightforward – two layers of fabric, with a layer of filling sandwiched between them, are stitched together. The stitch may be purely functional – to anchor the filling and prevent it from wandering about – or chosen to add to the decorative appeal of the work.

This practical method of quilting is still much in vogue for adding warmth and softness to everyday clothes and furnishings. However, more and more it is being used as a form of raised decoration in artwork, fashion design, and the home. It can be used on its own, or combined with other textile work, such as leatherwork, knitting and embroidery. It also combines excellently with other quilting techniques – with corded and stuffed quilting, for instance.

## Pattern and design (see also Chapter 1)

Since it was necessary to secure the wadding between the layers of fabric, original patterns were, by tradition, stitched in the familiar all-

over diagonal lines, diamonds and ogee. Of course it is important to stitch all over the wadded area to hold the layers together, but the pattern does not have to be a repetitive one – a quilted landscape is an example. Large unstitched areas must be avoided to prevent unwanted movement of wadding and fabrics. Equally, the stitching does not always want to be too close together either, for this produces a lower relief – stiffer and less warm – which flattens the work and reduces the puffy appearance.

Contour lines, like those on maps, lend themselves well to quilting on wadded materials. An attractive, all-over design consisting of random and meandering lines is easy to quilt, and requires little planning and no pattern to be transferred. One of the easiest ways of making a design is to use a printed fabric as a backing, and stitch round the pattern from the back. The print can be quite loud and gaudy, but if 'etched' round in thread to match or tone with the front material, the design can look most attractive on the front.

**22** Inspiration from maps and contour lines for all-over patterns for wadded quilting

**23** *Mendip.* Coarsely textured, loosely woven cheese cloth spray-painted in blues and greens along the wavy edges of cut-out card to resemble sky and hills. Wadded quilting finished with hand embroidery. 43cm by 36cm (17in by 14in). Anne Hulbert

Designs for wadded quilting should not be too intricate, or include a lot of short distances to be stitched, since this would involve too much to-ing and fro-ing, and this constant stopping and starting means a great many ends must be fastened off.

## Fabrics and fillings (see also Chapter 3)

Wadded quilting can be worked on a large range of types and textures of fabric. However, fabrics behave differently – for instance, woven man-made fabrics have little 'give', and do not, on the whole, quilt well. Soft, knitted materials work best of all – they give in all directions, and produce excellent relief. Commercially-printed fabrics are a help to those with little time or inclination to draw, since they already have their designs on them, and can be quilted on the front by simply tracing round the printed pattern.

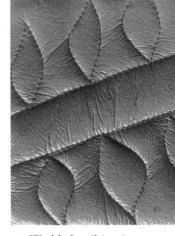

24 Wadded quilting in straight stitch on shiny stretch plastic. Anne Hulbert

25 *Strawberries*. Small panel with free-motion stitching on printed cotton sateen with a plastic foam padding and calico backing. Anne Hulbert

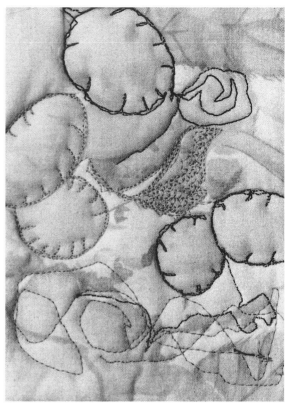

**26** Shoulder bag. Machine-embroidered wadded and corded quilting on an appealing 'Kate Greenaway' printed cotton. The lining is quilted in a trellis pattern appropriate to that in the printed design. The handle is finished with an automatic embroidery stitch. Anne Hulbert

**27** Wadded quilting with machine embroidery to emphasize an otherwise indistinct pattern on a printed cotton furnishing fabric. Anne Hulbert

The choice of padding must be governed by the intended purpose of the finished article, and requires careful thought. Garments will mainly require a soft, light and washable padding, whereas articles for furnishings will need a more substantial filling. Some (fortunately few) sewing machines are rather limited in the height they allow between the presser foot and the feed-dog, so do not give much room for thickly wadded quilting to be taken through. Check this before preparing the work to avoid later frustration and disappointment.

The weight and quality of a backing fabric for wadded quilting depends entirely on the nature of the top fabric. As a general rule, in order to ensure that the front of the work looks puffed up and well quilted, the backing should be slightly firmer than the front material in order to 'push' the padding upwards rather than to the underneath. If the reverse of the finished article is likely to be seen, it will need lining with a lightweight fabric to match, or tone with, the front material. This is to hide the 'workings'.

## Method of wadded quilting

Three layers of materials are required – the top (the front), the filling and the backing. The filling layer should be free from bumps and wrinkles. The other two layers must be ironed before they are quilted, as they cannot be ironed afterwards.

- Using one of the methods described in Chapter 1, transfer the design to the right side of the layer of material to be stitched.
- Sandwich the layer of wadding between the wrong sides of the top and backing layers (Fig 28).
- Tack the three layers together at regular intervals, starting at the centre and working outwards.

The following is a well-tried method of tacking which helps to prevent puckering. It takes a little longer but is well worth the time and effort spent.

- Cut the wadding to size and lay it flat on the work table.
- Cut the backing fabric slightly larger all round.
- Place the backing, right side up, over the wadding and pin or tape it down round the sides.
- Tack it to the wadding, carefully undoing the pins or tape as necessary to avoid too much disturbance of the two layers.
- Turn the two tacked layers over with the wadding uppermost and pin or tape them down on the table again round the sides.
- Lay the top fabric, right side up, over the wadding and tack through the three layers. The prepared materials are now ready to stitch.

Further details on tacking methods will be found in Chapter 4.

*Note*: Any work planned for the top fabric, such as appliqué, patchwork, other forms of quilting or fabric colouring, is usually completed prior to tacking it to the wadding and backing, and before quilting. This was particularly the case with the picture 'Rural Landscape' (Fig 90). The corded and stuffed quilting, and some of the free embroidery, were first worked on the top fabric backed with muslin. The piece was then backed with a layer of wadding and calico for further quilting.

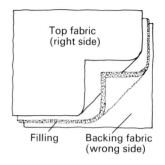

**28** The positioning of the three layers of materials for wadded quilting. The layer of filling is sandwiched between the wrong sides of the top and backing fabrics

## Threads and stitching (see also Chapter 4)

There is a great assortment of wonderfully coloured and textured threads available for machine stitching on layers of wadded fabrics. As with other methods of quilting, the finer ones can be threaded through the top system, and those that are too thick can be wound on the bobbin. Threads embedded in the puffy surface of quilting can look spectacular, particularly richly coloured silk and metallic. It is always an advantage to make a sampler with different threads on different wadded fabrics to see how they relate to each other – after all, the choice of thread must depend largely on its affinity with its padded background material.

Any manner of stitching can be used for wadded quilting – straight, satin, zig-zag, automatic patterns, free-motion embroidery, double or triple needle, and couching.

- Before commencing the stitching, reduce the pressure on the presser foot to enable the layers of fabrics, with the wadding, to pass through the machine easily. Too heavy a pressure on the bulky layers can inhibit the stitching process and wrinkle the fabrics.
- Loosen the top tension slightly and use a medium length stitch.

29 Sample of free-motion stitching on wadded calico using straight and zig-zag stitches. Anne Hulbert

**30** Bead-smocked waistcoast made from quilted silk. Before smocking the fabric was quilted all over in a diamond pattern with gold thread. The fabric for the collar, peplum and armhole are diagonally quilted with gold thread. Sue Rangeley

For very thickly wadded layers also loosen the bobbin tension a little, and use a longer stitch.

- Use a medium needle (size 80 to 90) for light quilting and a thicker needle (size 90 to 100 or 110) for quilting thicker layers of materials.

- If large articles of wadded quilting are cumbersome to manage in the machine, try to work with the the fabric mainly on the left. Then if necessary, roll up any on the right small enough to fit under the arm of the machine.

- It is better to stitch long straight lines across the grain of the fabric, rather than with it, to lessen the possibility of puckering; and stitching long straight pattern lines in opposite directions will also help.

- When the stitching has been completed take all thread ends through to the back and darn into the work, or tie in several

knots and trim to about 20mm ($\frac{3}{4}$in). Do not finish by reverse stitching: it always shows on the front.

- When all sewing is done remove the tackings and ease into shape. Line the work if necessary and make it up into the article planned.

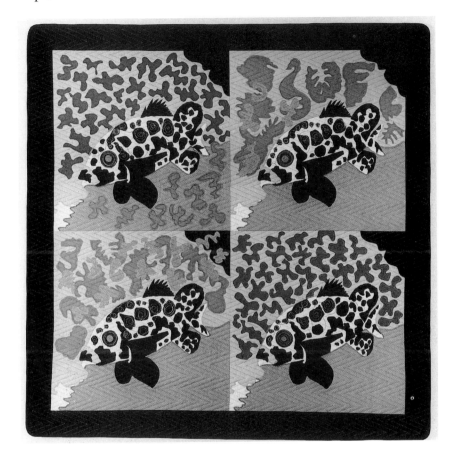

**31 (above)** *Sweetlips.* Cotton patchwork and appliqué quilt worked on an industrial machine. Pauline Burbidge

**32** Repetitive all-over patterns for stitching in long continuous lines

**33** *After the Storm*. A
sketch to paint on silk for
wadded quilting

**34** *Lowland Point*.
Watercolour painted on
calico and deeply quilted
with a plastic foam
wadding. The 'mount'
and the picture are one
piece of fabric. Rocks on
the foreshore are china
beads sewn on by hand.
The finished work was
stretched over thick card
to raise the padding
further. 25cm by 19cm
(10in by 7½in).
Anne Hulbert

**35** Early 19th century design for appliqué and embroidery, easily adapted for appliqué and wadded quilting

**36** *Duck on Lily Pond.* The head, neck and back of the duck are densely embroidered, stretched over card and hand stitched to the background (the white areas are left plain). The 'water' consists of hand-dyed silk, pleated, tucked and cord quilted. The lilies are cord quilted and appliquéd on, and have satin stitched stems and leaves. Black chiffon is used for shadow quilting to create the darker areas and trees. The free-standing reeds to the right are made from tapered strips of dyed silk, padded and satin stitched at the edges. The picture is backed with wadding prior to quilting. 58cm by 63cm (23in by 25in). Anna Donovan

**37** *Butterflies* picture. Hand painted on silk. Wadded quilting with silk threads in free-motion running stitch. 9cm by 11.5cm ($3\frac{1}{2}$in by $4\frac{1}{2}$in). Glenys Massey

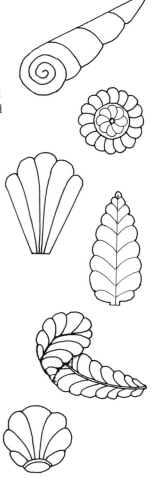

**38** A wavy border stencil spray-dyed across wadded calico and quilted. Note that spraying the fabric along the edges of the stencil heightens the padded effect. Anne Hulbert

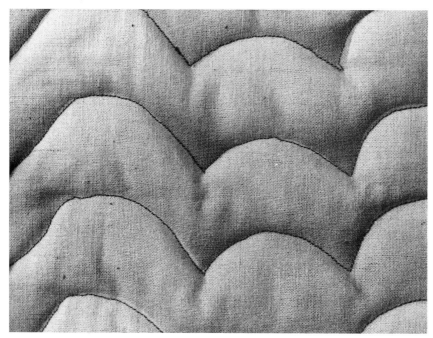

**39** These traditional hand quilting patterns could be worked quite easily with free-motion stitching

**40** Bird motif for a pocket, bag-front or for repeating round a quilt

**41** Ideas for motifs can be used from vegetables and fruit

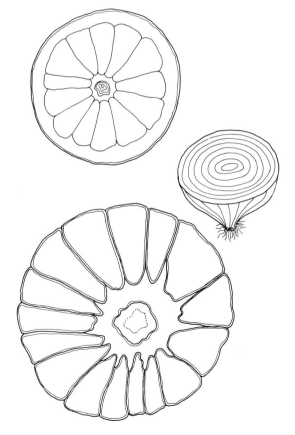

**42** Ideas for mixing wadded and corded quilting for children's garments

**43** Silk cushion with spray-dyed and stencilled design. The background is in wadded quilting stitched in random lines, and the flowers are quilted with satin stitch. Free-standing, cut-work butterflies and a little hand embroidery add a finish. Sue Rangeley

**44** Ideas for small quilted articles: mirror frame and book cover

**45** Silk cushion with spray-dyed flowers and leaves on a Chinese lattice background. The positive and the negative sections of the stencil can be used – one to spray the actual motif, and the other to screen the motif when spraying the area around it. Padded cut-work flowers and leaves add further interest.
Sue Rangeley

**46** Design for deck chair seat with plastic foam sandwiched between deck chair canvas and strong calico. Flower design to be painted or appliquéd prior to quilting, and the free-standing butterflies padded and edged with satin stitch

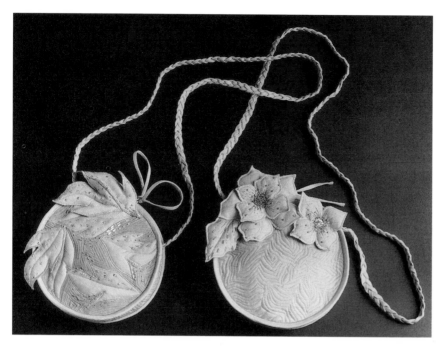

**47** *Bridal* pochettes. Each bag is made in natural ivory habutai silk worked in wadded quilting. The left-hand bag uses the quilting as a close-stitched background, leaving the leaf shapes plain and puffed up. The leaf shapes are repeated as free-standing cut-work padded motifs. The right-hand bag is close quilted all over, so less puffy, and finished with separate flowers. Both bags are trimmed with silk-bound edges and straps made from plaited silk rouleaux. Sue Rangeley

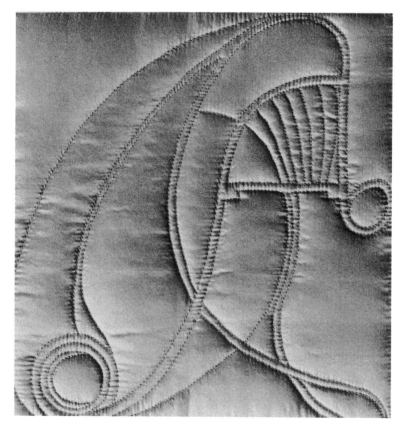

**48** Wadded panel in hand-dyed oyster coloured habutai silk. Art deco design worked in straight stitch with silk thread. 36cm by 33cm (14in by 13in). Anna Donovan

**49** Four pattern ideas for using singly, repeating in a block design over a large area, or as a border

**50** This design from a
Victorian tile would make
a pattern for wadded and
stuffed quilting combined

**52** Taken from a 1930s
embroidery, this design
could well be reproduced
in a combination of
wadded and stuffed
quilting

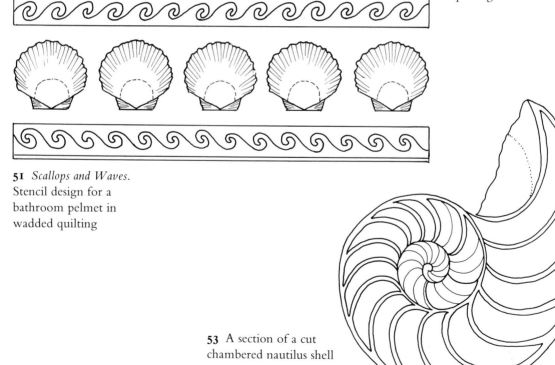

**51** *Scallops and Waves.*
Stencil design for a
bathroom pelmet in
wadded quilting

**53** A section of a cut
chambered nautilus shell

**54** The plan for making the seaside picture (Fig 55) with enlarged drawings, samples of fabric colours and textures and working notes. Anna Donovan

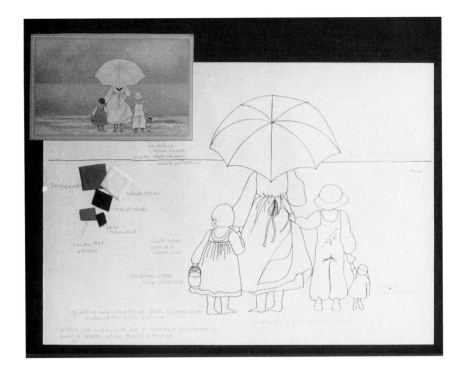

**55** *At the Seaside.* Inspired by a postcard, this sketch in fabric and thread combines several techniques on a wadded cotton background. The figures are appliquéd with Bondaweb, and the clothes flat quilted. The parasol struts are cord quilted by double needle, and the parasol made and padded separately. It is then appliquéd to the background with satin stitching. White wool is couched on and quilted to make the wave crests. Automatic stitch patterns are used to quilt the remaining waves and ripples. 53cm by 43cm (21in by 17in). Anna Donovan

**56** *Pond Life* jacket in shades of sludgy green velvet and silk. The wide painted silk welt is worked in wadded and corded quilting in straight and satin stitches and, like the cuffs, is finished with an automatic pattern. The lilies and their centres are padded and cut-worked separately, and attached by hand. Each stem is a rouleau – a turned, stitched hollow tube. The front edges and armhole seams are also finished with an automatic stitch. Anna Donovan

**57** *Brick* jacket. Sprayed cotton jacket worked in wadded quilting. The material was coloured prior to cutting out and making up. Karoline O'Neill

**1** Quilted accessories to liven up a bedroom – a
spray-dyed padded cut-work tie-back, painted and
quilted silk cushions and a sprayed and painted silk
bedspread. The cut-work butterflies on the
bedspread were repeated and painted on the curtain.
Sue Rangeley

**2** A wall-hanging using wadded quilting on spray-dyed and splattered silk. Areas are masked to build up the design gradually with varying depths of colour. Diana Harrison

**3** *Summer Border* – fabric wall-hanging. The flowers were made from different sizes of stuffed pompon, with smaller versions reversed, and assorted beads as the centres. The stalks were worked in 'pad-as-you-go' quilting. The trees and hedging were machine quilted, or beaded, and made separately before stitching them in place by machine or by hand. The 'bound edge' method of finishing was used to make the frame, but with thick, bouncy wadding to complete the overall padded effect. 66cm by 60cm (26in by 24in). Anne Hulbert

**4** Silk screen. Spray-dyed and stencilled floral design worked in wadded quilting. Free-standing butterflies are wadded with cut-work edges in close satin stitch. Sue Rangeley

**5** *Country House.* Appliqué and patchwork hanging worked in wadded quilting with plain and textured fabrics using zig-zag, satin and embroidery stitching. Barbara Duncan

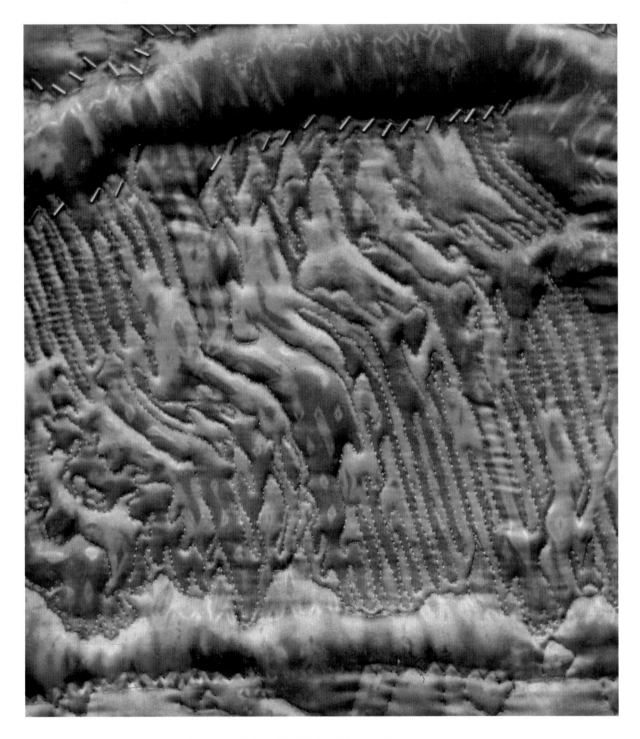

**6** *Atlantic Rollers*. Wadded quilting on silk satin.
Resist dyed, with machine embroidery worked
with hand-dyed silk threads. 58cm by 64cm (23in by
25in). Vivien Prideaux

7 Silk fan. Hand painted irises and their leaves stand out remarkably on the painted background of this delicate silk fan. The background and the irises are worked in wadded quilting with free-motion stitching. Vivien Prideaux

8 Small, hand-dyed panel using double needle cording on wadded silk as a background for free-standing padded flowers and machine embroidered padded appliqué. Anna Donovan

**9** A collection of quilted cushions. Clockwise from bottom centre: (a) corded lattice patterns worked with a double needle on heavy cotton sateen; (b) single and double needle cording and pin-tucking combined with wadded quilting on silk patchwork; (c) all-over corded trellis design worked on wadded rayon stain; (d) three diamond-shaped panels of 'pad-as-you-go' joined to form a hexagon; (e) single needle quilting along the seams of wadded log-cabin patchwork; (f) stuffed quilted birds with corded tails on commercially printed furnishing cotton; (g) interwoven bands of single needle cording, alternating the right and wrong side of dupion.
Anne Hulbert

**10** *Victorian Tile* wall plaque. The idea for the centre panel was taken from an old tile and worked on gold gloving kid backed with firm cotton. The pattern was drawn on the front of the leather with an H pencil and stitched from the front. Four forms of quilting were used: (a) flat, for the background design and inner border in zig-zag and satin stitch; (b) corded, for the flower stems and tile border; (c) stuffed, for the tulips; and (d) wadded, for the stretch velvet frame worked in free-motion stitching with a plastic foam filling. 37cm (14½in) square. Anne Hulbert

**11** A colourful tabard. Wadded quilting on vibrantly dyed silks. The leaves are a padded cut-work version of the bold and beautiful indoor plant *Monstera Deliciosa*. Vivien Prideaux

**12** *Fairground.* Flat quilted nursery rug made of hand-made and hand-dyed felt. The felt was backed with a firm plain cotton which supports its weight and prevents it from stretching. The design was outlined and decorated with free-motion embroidery stitches through both layers. The rug was lined with a non-slip material.
Karen McCormac

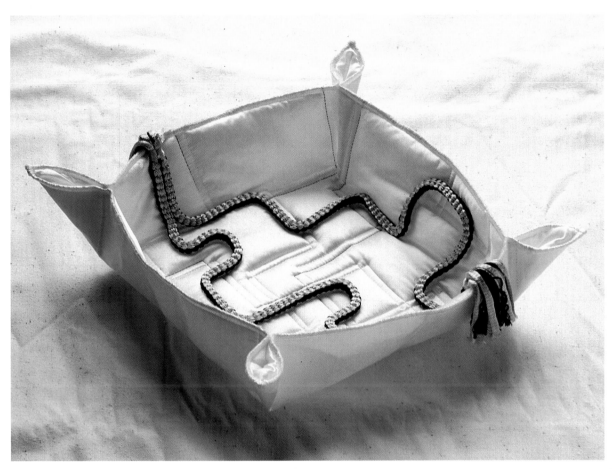

**13** Habutai silk bowl. Corded and wadded quilting are used. Decorated with Japanese silk plait and tassel. Vivien Prideaux

**14** Padded silk flowers. The flowers were spray-dyed and hand-painted prior to cutting out. They were backed with wadding and a backing fabric, and satin-stitched round the edges in silver and gold metallic threads. Beads were sewn on in the centres. Sue Rangeley

**15** Elegant tie-backs for curtains using various methods of padding and quilting. From the top: (a) 'Pad–as–you–go' in cream, beige and pink polyester satin; (b) Wadded flowers and leaves, in one piece, were taken from printed glazed chintz. Cut-worked edges were closely satin stitched. The leaves were made separately and hand-sewn in place; (c) Wadded printed furnishing cotton with a padded rosette, and satin stitched edges. Sections of the pattern on the fabric were cut out and rearranged to make a symmetrical form; (d) Wadded dupion with free-standing and appliquéd butterflies that were cut from the curtain material. Beads and sequins were used for features; (e) Narrow wadded strip of spray-dyed ivy leaves with satin stitched edges. Anne Hulbert

**16** Shot silk antung jacket decorated with double needle simulated cording. Note how increased bobbin thread tension throws up the pattern well on a soft fabric. Bead embroidery and cut-work collar and cuffs. Vivien Prideaux

**17** Cord quilted panel. Wide channels of single needle stitching on loosely-woven domette with muslin backing. Corded with frayed strips of red and black chiffon, and white quilting wool. The loops left at intersections on the right side form part of the design. Claire Helen Johnson

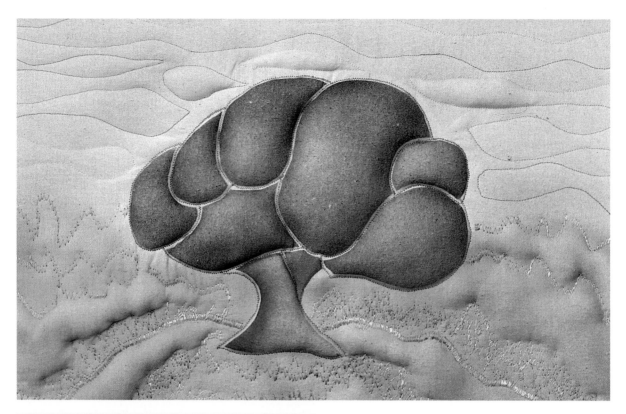

**18** *Great Oak*. Calico panel worked with mixed techniques. The stencilled design is first worked in wadded quilting – random stitching on the sky and free-motion stitching over the foreground. The tree and a few clouds were further heightened by inserting extra filling into the backs of the motifs. Knolls were formed by stuffing areas among the freely stitched patterns. 25cm by 30cm (10in by 12in). Anne Hulbert

**19** *Objets Trouvés*. Panel. The design was spray-dyed through stencil cut-outs on to soft calico, and backed with heavier calico. The stonework background was flat-quilted with free-motion zig-zag stitching through both layers. The nautilus was outlined in straight stitch, and the sections divided with tapering widths of satin stitch to give greater sense of depth. Variegated rayon threads were used throughout. It was stuffed from the back to a height of 2.5cm (1in) at the fattest part. Natural shells were glued to the foreground. 36cm by 43cm (14in by 17in). Anne Hulbert

**20** *Pear Tree*. Shadow-worked habutai silk panel with a calico backing. The fruit and leaves were effectively stuffed with mixed shades of strongly-coloured chopped wools to simulate their natural appearance. Finished with glass and silver beads, and hand embroidery. 40cm by 36cm (16in by 14in). Anne Hulbert

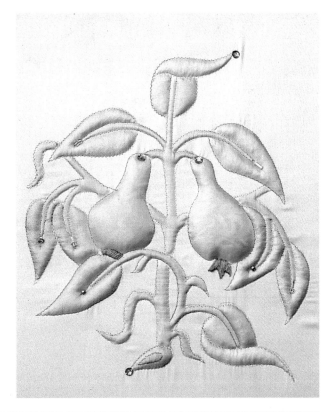

**21** A collection of quilted and padded boxes. The fabrics were prepared in sections – dyed, painted, patched, embroidered and quilted – before being joined together to make into boxes. Jacky Cook and Claire Johnson

**22** Two silk cord-quilted and shadow-worked cushions. Left, *Stripes Within a Frame*. The required amount of white habutai silk was stitched, with a double needle, to a muslin backing and corded with very brightly coloured knitting yarns. The finished piece was then cut into four triangles and re-assembled to make the panel, and bordered with plain silk. Right, *Trellis and Triangles*. Pairs of diagonal parallel rows of single needle stitching are worked on fine cream silk twill, with wadding and backing muslin behind. Very bright insertions were threaded through the channels to create delicate fondant-like 'shadows'. Squares folded into triangles form the border. Tiny pearl beads were added at the junctions. Anne Hulbert

**23** Dressing gown. Bands of soft cotton lawn are stitched together to make pieces of material large enough for each section of the garment. They were backed with wadding and muslin, then quilted vertically down the seams on the right side. Caroline Hooper

**24** Luxurious bed-head made of many padded and quilted flowers and leaves cut out of the curtain material. Time- and thread-consuming, but well worth the outlay for both. Length 200cm (78in). Anne Hulbert

**25** *Cavalier* – padded appliqué picture. The dog design was sprayed through a series of stencils on to silk, and quilted with wadding and a backing fabric. The leather nose and gold kid collar, gold chain beads and glass bead eyes were sewn on by hand. The work was outlined in zig-zag stitch, and the surplus layers of material were cut away close to the stitching. The dog was then tacked and satin stitched to the velvet ground. Two rows of thick cord and gold bobbles and braid made up the frame. The finished work was mounted on to thin plywood. 40cm by 51cm (15½in by 20in). Anne Hulbert and Sue Rangeley

**26** *Acorn* – a spectacular arrangement of dyed and painted silk acorns and oak leaves. The wadded leaves were quilted and edged with close zig-zag covering fine wire to give them support and flexibility. The acorns were made by stuffing the shapes, and the 'cups' by covering polystyrene shapes with ruched silk. Heavy wire was bound with silk to make the branches. Height 120cm (48in). Jackie Anderson, for Manuel Canovas

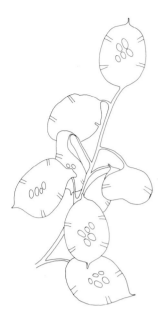

**58** Honesty seed–pods are a versatile old favourite used for textile designs, particularly quilting

**59** Exotic flower jacket from Thailand. Hand-painted silk with very vividly coloured flowers on a black ground. Worked in wadded quilting, outlining each flower. The front band, collar and cuffs are straight stitched

**60** Cotton quilt worked in wadded strip-patchwork. The completed squares of strips are backed with wadding and joined on the right side. The seams are then covered with bands of material sewn on with zig-zag stitch. Anne Murphy

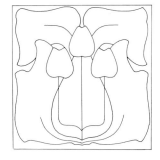

# Flat Quilting

**61** Design of a Victorian tile. This was used for the wall-plaque (see colour section) incorporating flat quilting with other quilting methods

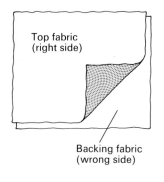

Top fabric
(right side)

Backing fabric
(wrong side)

**62** The arrangement of the two layers of fabric

Flat quilting is, quite simply, the stitching together of two pieces of fabric in a decorative fashion without the addition of any kind of filling. Its character lies mainly in the aesthetic effect provided by the stitching. Without wadding to create the extra dimension, the stitched line is all-important and needs emphasis. Thicker and more textured threads, rather than the usual everyday sewing threads, are therefore used, and careful consideration given to their selection.

It might be argued that, in appearance, this form of quilting resembles top stitching more than conventional quilting. Nevertheless, although only two layers of material are used, they do make a degree of padding for each other.

Flat quilting can be most useful for adding textural interest, strength and substance and a little extra warmth, without additional bulk, to vulnerable areas of articles of clothing, particularly collars, cuffs and pocket edges. About the house, it can be used to provide weight and firmness to tablemats, curtain borders and hems, and light-weight bed-coverlets.

It also combines beautifully with other quilting worked with only two layers of fabric. Such decoration greatly enhances the flat areas between hummocks of stuffed quilting (trapunto), or between widely-spaced channels in corded quilting.

## Pattern and design (see also Chapter 1)

Because the interest provided by flat quilting lies in the contrast between the rich texture of the stitching and the area of background

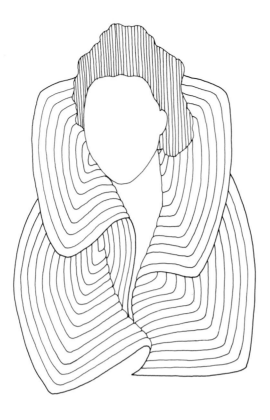

**63** Design for a flat quilted large collar. Both layers of fabric require a degree of stiffness to hold the shape, and the stitching needs to be well spaced

fabric, simple patterns are the most suitable, particularly linear and geometric forms. Repetitive, all-over 'filling' patterns and border designs are well-suited to this technique. So too is a meandering pattern, which is simply continuous random stitching over an area, with few stops and starts – the design being invented as the work progresses.

Most of the traditional patterns used for other methods of quilting may be used for flat quilting. The design can be marked on the right side of the top fabric (before tacking) and stitched from the front, or marked on the right side of the backing fabric and stitched from the back.

**64** *Charleston Girl* – motif for a pocket or bag-flap

## Fabrics (see also Chapter 3)

The top, or front layer of fabric should be the better quality, whereas the backing, though it should be of much the same weight and thickness, can be of a lesser quality. Should stiffness be required, an

**65** (above) A combination of flat quilting with stuffed raised areas could be created from this Art Deco tile design

**66** (above right) Linear pattern suitable for a pocket or bag-flap

iron-on or a sew-in non-woven interlining (available in different weights) makes an excellent backing, as it is easy to work and the design lines can be marked clearly on the back. Any of the very wide variety of materials that the sewing machine can cope with may be used for flat-quilted projects, including leather, suede, synthetics and plastics. It is, however, important to experiment first with different fabrics and threads to ensure that the finished article is perfect.

Seldom reversible, the flat-quilted piece of work will almost always need to be lined to protect the threads and joins at the back, and to conceal pattern lines and the wrong side of the stitching. The choice of lining fabric depends entirely on the purpose of the article to be made. It may match or contrast in colour, pattern or texture with the fabric used for the quilting and, as it is likely to be visible, its selection will need careful consideration.

## Method of flat quilting (see Fig 62)

- Iron the top and backing fabrics before transferring the design – to the right side of either layer.
- Tack both layers firmly together.
- Stitch along the pattern lines throughout the entire design. There is a wide variety of coloured and textured threads

suitable for flat quilting. The finer ones can be threaded through the top system, and the thicker ones wound on the bobbin and stitched from the wrong side. Bulky threads can always be couched on to the right side of the work with the help of the braiding or cording presser foot.

- On no account use reverse stitching to finish off this work – it would look untidy and unprofessional. Always take the thread ends to the back and darn them into the fabric.
- Remove the tacking stitches and line the work accordingly.

When flat quilting is to be combined with wadded or corded quilting, which are both worked on two layers of fabric, its stitching must be completed before the filling is inserted. It would be very difficult to work the stitching afterwards.

**67** Dark green suede jacket with flat quilting on the collar, cuffs, welt and the front. The leaves, although simulating appliqué, were outlined with pale green silk thread in graduating satin stitch, with straight stitched veins. Throughout the garment the edges of the suede were finished with satin stitched cut-work. Karoline O'Neill

**68** Design for a child's dress with flat quilting worked on bodice and round the hem

**69** (above right) Design for a kimono to be flat quilted in free-motion embroidery with shaded silk threads on silk satin

**70** Ideas for flat quilting borders, panels, and motifs from Chinese and other sources

**71** *Golden Eagle*. Small flat-quilted picture worked on a ready-printed heavy furnishing cotton backed with iron-on Vilene. Free-motion embroidery and couching marked throughout using Madeira gold metallic, shaded rayon threads and cotton perle. 14cm by 19cm (5½in by 7½in). Anne Hulbert

**72** *Golden Eagle*. Reverse of Fig 71 showing the back of the piece and demonstrating how a printed material can effectively be used as a pattern for a design. It was applied to the back, and stitched from the back to produce a more delicate pattern than on the original print. A help to the non-artistic! Anne Hulbert

**73** *Entrada*. One of a set of flat quilted mats. Non-woven iron-on interlining was used to back the textured linen front. The design was marked on the back, and stitched from the back, through both layers. A thickish Lyscordet (no. 5) crochet cotton wound on the bobbin produced the bold stitching on the front. It was worked in varying lengths of straight and zig-zag, giving a couched effect. Normal sewing thread was used for the top and needle system. The mat was lined with calico and finished with close satin stitch all round. 18cm by 21cm (7in by 8½in). Anne Hulbert

**74** *City Horizon* – large border design

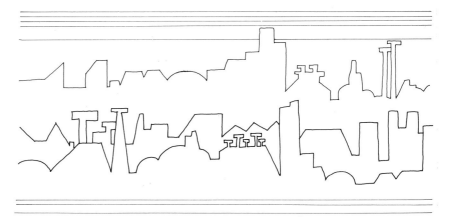

# CHAPTER 7

# Corded Quilting

Purists might argue that this aspect of quilting is not, in fact, quilting. However, decorating fabrics for clothes and domestic articles with raised linear designs has, beyond doubt, been regarded for some centuries as an important method of quilting. Hitherto known as 'Italian' quilting, this technique is today more often referred to in textbooks and classrooms as 'corded' quilting.

The designs are based on parallel lines and can be worked by machine on a double or single layer of fabric – with or without a filling. On a double layer, the lines are stitched through both fabrics to form channels, through which one or more strands of 'cord' are threaded to raise the pattern into relief.

A single, double, or triple needle may be used. However, it is the use of a double or triple needle that makes it possible to produce corded quilting and simulated corded quilting very quickly on a single layer of fabric.

This form of quilting is easier to manoeuvre through the sewing machine than wadded quilting. There is less bulk to handle because the filling is inserted after the stitching has been completed.

Corded quilting is a handsome and versatile form of fabric decoration; but, unlike wadded quilting, there is less padding so it cannot provide the same insulation. Hence it is used mainly for its decorative appearance on garments and household articles, rather than for warmth. In the fashion world, corded quilting will always retain a popular elegance, and eye-catching as well as practical designs can be created to suit almost any garment, trimming or accessory. It can be useful too, for providing stiffness to collars, cuffs and fabric hat-brims. All manner of articles for the home can be

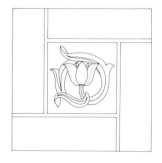

**75** An Art Deco tile with a design suitable for corded quilting

**76** Suggestions for using
corded quilting on
garments and accessories

**77** Corded quilting raised with a soft acrylic yarn insertion on habutai silk cravat. It started as a simple corded band, and folded into this form. Single needle stitching. Phyllis Ross

**78** Cord quilted motif on polyester satin pocket. Single needle stitching with varying channel widths. Anne Hulbert

**79** Cushion. Cord quilting combined with stuffed quilting on printed furnishing cotton. The channels in the birds' tails vary in width and were raised by cording. Beads sewn to eyes and flower centres. Single needle stitching. Border of patchworked velvet. Anne Hulbert

greatly enlivened with cord-quilted patterns, as all-over designs or simple single motifs.

Corded quilting combines beautifully with all the other quilting methods, to fill in a background or to outline and emphasize single motifs in a design. Mastering the technique will amply repay the effort expended, for it offers a seemingly endless variety of interesting, unusual and elegant effects.

## Pattern and design (see also Chapter 1)

Patterns founded on uniformly stitched parallel lines seem to demand a certain formality in their planning. And because of the nature of corded quilting, plus the fact that it is being worked on the sewing machine, the designs must be kept simple. The channels can be varied in width and plumpness, and they can be curved and serpentine as well as straight. Plan them to be as long and continuous as possible, in order to avoid having to stop and restart in the middle – joins in the stitching spoil the work, and they can weaken the area. Since the patterns consist of two lines of stitching, it is usually only necessary to mark one of them on to the fabric – the distance for the second line can easily be gauged by stitching with the edge of the presser foot on the first line. The distance between rows of stitching can also be varied by moving the needle to the right or left of its normal central position.

## Fabrics and fillings (see also Chapter 3)

While the majority of fabrics recommended for the top, backing and lining of machine-quilted pieces are equally suitable for corded work, there are a few exceptions. Very rough, coarsely-woven fabrics are best avoided for the front of the work, since they do not generally make for sharp, clear edges to raised linear patterns, and such textures can detract from the actual cording. Boldly-printed fabrics, particularly those with large, bright and busy patterns, do not qualify either. A good, well-worked design of raised lines is 'lost' if it cannot be distinguished from its background. Except in special circumstances, stiff heavy fabrics are unsuitable for the front or back of corded quilting. Such fabrics are generally difficult to handle, and it can be quite laborious to pull insertion cords through the stitched channels. Moreover, the end result tends to be stiff and solid.

The most important requirement for front and backing fabrics for corded quilting is that the cording yarn can be properly inserted and threaded through the stitched channels without difficulty.

The filling for corded quilting – whatever it might be – must always be as compatible with the fabric housing it, as with the purpose of the article being made. Experiment as much as possible with different colours and textures and a variety of fabrics, and make sure sufficient quantities of those selected can be maintained to complete the work.

## Methods of corded quilting

### Using a single needle

Two layers of material are required: a front and a backing. They should be well ironed before use, since they cannot be satisfactorily ironed after quilting.

- Using one of the methods described in Chapter 1 transfer the design to the right side of the layer to be stitched.
- Pin and tack the front and backing fabrics together with wrong sides facing.
- Set the machine for a medium length straight stitch and adjust top and bobbin tensions to suit the threads.
- Starting at, or near, the centre when possible, stitch along the marked lines of the design. While it is usually more practical to complete the stitching round one set of lines before embarking on the second, the order of working really depends on the design. It may, in some instances, be easier to finish both lines in one area before moving to the next. When the stitching lines for two channels have to cross each other, raise the needle and presser foot and ease the work forward. Doing this will ensure a clear passage for the cord – stitches across the channels would prevent the cord getting through (see Fig 80).
- Fasten all thread ends off at the back and remove the tacking stitches.
- Thread the bodkin, or blunt-ended needle, with the selected cord, not too long; about 50cm (20in) is enough at a time.
- Always insert the cord from the back of the work. Ease the weave of the backing fabric apart and pass the needle and cord

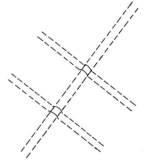

**80** Advancing the stitch to cross the first stitched channel

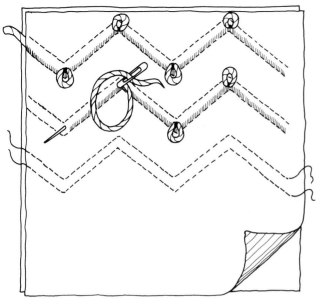

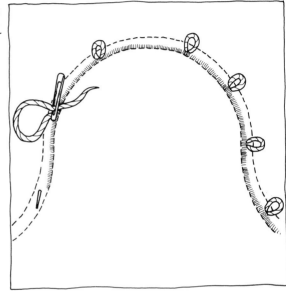

**81** Inserting the cord, with loops left at sharp angles

**82** Inserting the cord, with loops left at curved areas

into the stitched channel. Draw them through, leaving an end of 12mm ($\frac{1}{2}$in) to allow the cord some 'give' within the channel. Do not pull the filling too tight: it will cause the quilting to wrinkle, and should the work be stretched it would be too short in its channel, leaving 'pockets' with no filling.

● At curves and corners, the needle and cord are brought out and re-inserted in the same hole, leaving a 12mm ($\frac{1}{2}$in) loop. This also relieves the tension of the cord, and prevents it from puckering the work (see Figs 81 and 82).

● Should, by any chance, the channels have been stitched across the intersections, in either or both directions, the cords must be crossed outside the channels, at the back. Simply bring the needle out on one side of the intersection and re-insert on the opposite side. Do the same with the cord in the channel running across in the other direction (see Fig 83).

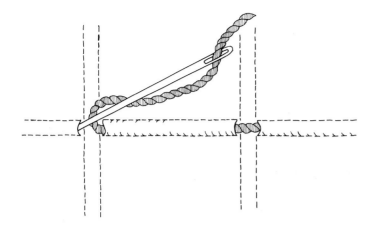

- The corded method of quilting can also be used to fill long shapes of variable widths – tapering leaves and tail feathers of birds for example. Lengths of cord are taken in and out of the shape at different points to lie side by side, forming a graduated outline (see Fig 84). It is considerably easier to fill such shapes by this method, rather than trying to fill them evenly with little wads of stuffing.
- After completing the cording of all the channels in the work, trim the ends to about 12mm ($\frac{1}{2}$in) and, if possible, unravel a little to avoid them appearing lumpy from the front.
- Finally, before making up into an article, stretch the piece very gently in different directions to 'settle' the tension of the cording, and to minimise wrinkles.

The lines of designs for corded quilting do not always need to be worked in straight stitch. Experiment with zig-zag and the decorative automatic patterns – they can look quite spectacular running along beside the raised channels. Try them with threads in variegated colours, or bright and lively metallic threads. And a delicate pale silk fabric stitched with a matching thread can be wonderfully subtle. For zig-zag stitching use the general purpose foot, but for the automatic patterns use the embroidery foot: the groove underneath allows extra height for the thickness of the close-worked stitches.

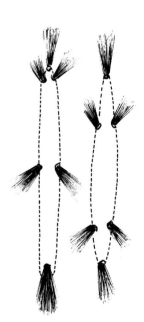

**84** Filling an elongated tapered shape using different lengths of yarn

### Using a double needle
It is possible to stitch and fill the channels on a single layer of fabric in one operation by using a double needle with one of the special presser

**85** (below) Corded quilting on soft leather. Single and double needle stitching. Wavy automatic pattern stitched with double needle. Anne Hulbert

**86** (below right) Cording used to gather a fabric. Cord was inserted in the same operation as double needle stitching on heavy dupion, and drawn to produce fullness. Anne Hulbert

feet. The foot required is either a cording foot, an underbraider or a raised attachment, according to the make of machine (consult the manufacturer's handbook). Some machines have a special hole in the needle plate through which to bring the cord up. In all cases the cord is held in a groove on the underside of the presser foot, and guided through the machine under the fabric. The reverse of double needle sewing is similar to zig-zag, and it is within this stitching that the cord is secured at the back of the work.

The thickness of the cord that can be used for this work is determined by the presser foot, and the size of its groove. As a rule there is only room for quite a fine yarn – crochet cotton, size 3–5, and gimps and yarns of similar size work very well.

Stitching with a double needle, combined with the presence of the cord during the stitching, makes it difficult to cope with sharp corners and intricate patterns: the cord can slip out of its channel. But for large and simple projects this is a fast and straightforward way of cord-quilting.

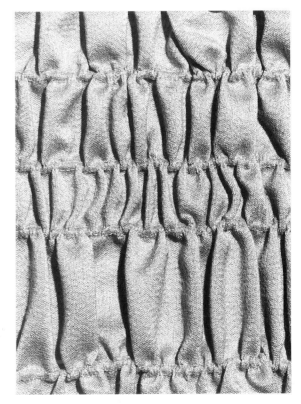

The width of the channel is constant once the needle is fitted – it can only be varied by changing the needle for a wider, or narrower gauge.

The height of the cording can be raised or lowered by increasing or lowering the top tension. And using a darker thread in one needle will give the impression of greater depth in the quilting.

An interesting effect can be achieved by stitching rows of narrow gauged double needle cording about 1cm ($\frac{1}{2}$in) apart, and threading a plumper filling, by hand, between them. Try this with coloured fillings on fine chiffon.

Corded quilting can also be most useful for gathering material where fullness is required on a largish scale (see Fig 86). When the filling cord is inserted, either by hand or by machine, it is not caught by the stitches. It can then be drawn up, thus gathering the fabric on which it is worked. If more than one row is stitched, filled and gathered, it then becomes decorative as well as useful for pelmets and bed valances, and also, for articles of clothing.

## Simulated cording

This is the simplest and the fastest method of producing 'corded' quilting. Again, it is worked with a double needle, but with no

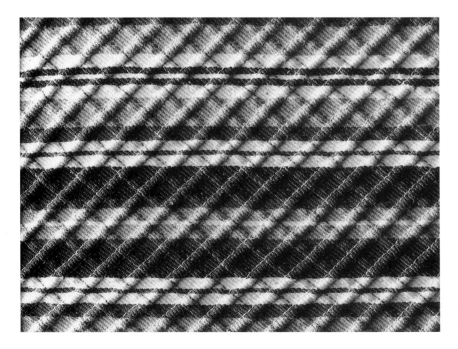

**87** Stitching and cord insertion worked in one operation with double needle and pin-tuck foot, on striped cotton twill. Anne Hulbert

**88** Simulated cording
worked on stretch velvet
with double needle and
increased bobbin tension.
No filling. Anne Hulbert

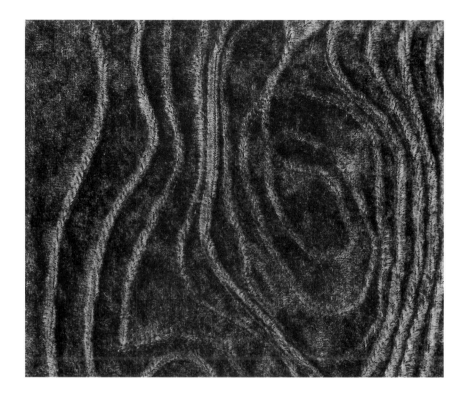

filling. Just fit the needle, thread the two threads, fill the bobbin and
adjust the top and bottom tensions – the more the top tension is
increased, the higher the 'cording' will appear to be.

Simulated cording works marvellously on soft, stretchy materials
with plenty of 'give'. Knitted jersey, rather than woven fabrics, is
ideal. Such 'ghost' cording is an excellent way of embroidering a
large area quickly. And if a soft, lightweight material is used the piece
is unlikely to end up over-stiff, because there it has no cord to make it
so!

When cord-quilting something large like an entire garment or a
bed covering, it is more satisfactory to quilt, at the outset, sufficient
fabric from which to cut all the necessary pieces. This is simpler than
cutting out each piece in a larger size to allow for quilting 'take-up',
and then having to work the cording to match on corresponding
pieces of the article.

Cord-quilted pieces will almost always need lining before making
up to protect the back of the work, to cover the untidiness, and to
give a professional appearance. The lining can match or contrast with
the front material or, if unseen, can be made of an oddment of
lightweight cotton.

**89** *Lowland Point.* Seascape worked with single and double needle stitching on cream habutai silk. The rocks are small china beads. Channels threaded with soft wool yarn. 41cm by 36cm (16in by 14in). Anne Hulbert

**90** *Rural Landscape.* Sampler of quilting techniques worked on polyester satin. Ploughed fields and trees were stuffed and corded prior to mounting the piece on to a wadded backing. Quilting was then worked round trees and hedges. Additional decoration of bead and machine embroidery. 63cm by 51cm (25in by 20in). Anne Hulbert and Diana Thornton

**91** Cotton jacket. Double
needle simulated cording.
Increased bobbin tension.
No filling. Yoke and
collar cording finished
with beads.
Anna Donovan

**92** Corded quilting used
as a background for a
stuffed motif. Cording
also outlines the motif.
Single needle stitching on
slubbed cotton.
Diana Thornton

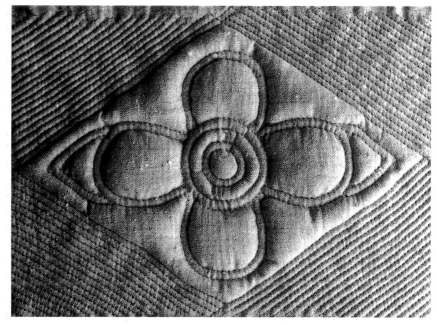

**93** *Arches*. Large habutai silk hanging. Bands of cord quilted silk threaded into a corded silk background. Single needle stitching. Phyllis Ross

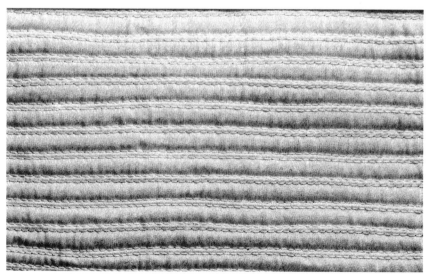

**94** Shadow cording. Pairs of lines were stitched across a fine, muslin-backed, habutai silk using a 1.5mm double needle. Bright-coloured tapisserie wools were threaded through the channels between the pairs of lines to produce a delicately striped effect. Anne Hulbert

**95** Cording on muslin-backed heavy Dralon velvet – diagonal lines with a double needle and horizontal lines with a single needle. The cord was threaded through channels between the pairs of double needle stitching, but between each line of single needle stitching

**96** (right) Motifs, borders and all-over patterns from various ancient and modern design sources, including Indian, Islamic, Chinese, Prehistoric and late 19th Century Art Nouveau

**97** Bronze lurex jacket with appliquéd motifs on the shoulders. Double needle simulated corded quilting on the front and upper sleeves. No filling. Vivien Prideaux

**98** A Victorian tile design suitable for combining corded and stuffed quilting in the same work

# CHAPTER 8

# Stuffed Quilting

**99** *Daffodils*. Art Deco tile with a design most suitable for stuffed quilting

Known also as trapunto, stuffed quilting has been used to add areas of raised decoration to garments and household articles for a very long time. In the Victoria and Albert Museum in London there is a Sicilian quilt of the late 14th century that is lavishly embroidered with areas of stuffed quilting depicting the Legend of Tristram. The work demonstrates a vast range of padded motifs worked in meticulous detail. It was, of course, hand-stitched, but nevertheless it is full of inspiration for working stuffed quilting on the sewing machine. Nowadays, stuffed quilting is used more for its decorative appearance than for keeping warm. Unless very lightweight fillings were used to pad out the pattern, garments and bed covers would be too thick and heavy for comfort and cleaning.

Stuffed quilting adds a third dimension to an otherwise flat surface by emphasizing certain areas of its design, and at the same time making maximum use of light and shade. The method is very much akin to corded quilting, in that the design is stitched through two layers of fabric and filled from the back after completion of the stitching. However, instead of being based on parallel lines, the patterns consist of simple individual shapes outlined by stitching, prior to raising with a filling.

While not the quickest form of quilting, it is certainly one of the most attractive, producing a considerably greater relief than can be attained using other techniques.

Machine stitching is most suitable for stuffed quilting – its closeness and durability provide the necessary strength to bear the strain of separately padded mounds on a flat background.

The high relief, and sculptural effects created by stuffed quilting

**100** Stuffed and corded quilting on a sun-dress bodice

89

are especially suitable for highlighting particular areas on garments and fashion accessories: for example, waistcoats, collars, cuffs, pockets, dress hems, dress yokes, glove backs, handbag flaps and belts.

In the home, individually padded shapes can add considerable interest to room décor, and re-vitalize quite everyday articles practically and economically. Stuffed quilting looks most attractive on pelmets, bed-canopies, curtain tie-backs, cushions, stool and chair seats; also on wall panels and artwork hangings.

Careful thought should be given to the use of stuffed quilting for all-over patterns. A large number of individually stuffed motifs might add much weight and bulk to articles like quilts and coats – lightweight fabrics and filling are essential for such articles.

Stuffed quilting is also well suited to border designs. Plait, scroll and cable patterns can be made into unusual frames to further enliven quilted and embroidered pictures. Being closely related in their techniques, stuffed and corded quilting will always complement each other and look good together – both are frequently included in the same piece. The padded hummocks contrast most agreeably with the sharpness and uniformity of raised linear designs. It is also an

**101** *Puff Ball* jacket made from spray-dyed and stencilled cotton. Raised circles were stitched, using free-motion stitching, stuffed and sewn up again entirely on the right side. Karoline O'Neill

**102** Design for a bag combining stuffed, wadded and corded quilting

90

**103** Idea for a child's jacket with stuffed cat motifs across the back, and corded quilting at the neck, cuffs and welt

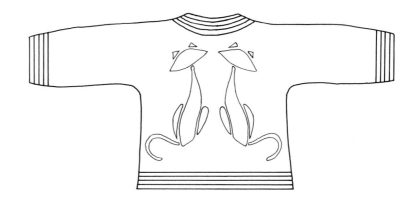

**104** *Arum.* Stuffed, corded and wadded shadow-quilting worked on off-white silk satin. The background consists of a layer of satin over a layer of very bright green shiny glazed chintz, with a layer of wadding behind. Metallic silver and shaded metallic threads, using straight, narrow satin and zig-zag stitches, outline the design through the three thicknesses. All the motifs were raised by inserting the filling between the front satin and the chintz. The firmness of the chintz throws the filled flower and leaves well forward, enhancing their fine forms greatly. The arum flower was padded with a pure white synthetic filling, and the leaves and stalks with chopped acrylic yarn in several shades of green. Detailing worked with beads and hand embroidery. 28cm by 36cm (11in by 14in). Anne Hulbert

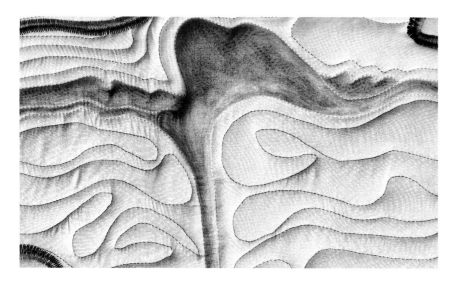

**105** Silk panel with spray-dyed stuffed design combined with wadded quilting. Background of random stitching in shaded metallic thread. 28cm by 18cm (11in by 7in). Anna Donovan

interesting way of adding further relief to work already quilted by other methods.

Stuffed quilting can be used to great effect on a variety of materials that have already been embellished by other techniques – for example, materials which have been spray-dyed, painted, embroidered, appliquéd, or patched, or which are commercially printed. It can also add extra interest to knitted and crocheted garments.

Because of the nature of the quilting, the designs are best limited to softly rounded outlines for easy filling and moulding. It is difficult to push the stuffing into the sharp corners of angular patterns.

## Fabrics and fillings (see also Chapter 3)

On the whole most of the top fabrics suggested for machine quilting are suitable for the stuffed method. However, any 'knitted' material with plenty of stretch can be raised and moulded far more easily than a firm woven one with no 'give'. And high relief can be achieved. Natural fibres like silk and calico pad out well, and silk, particularly, catches the light beautifully.

When combining shadow work with stuffed quilting, use semi-transparent and very fine fabrics with some 'give' – the higher the contours, the more the colours of the filling will show.

As discussed earlier, there is a wonderful variety of filling materials to choose from for padding individual shapes for traditional, as well

**106** *Poppies*. Panel of stuffed flowers with single needle stitching. Cord-filled stems stitched with double needle. Flower centres coloured with brown permanent marker. Brown stitching on cream calico. 38cm (15in) square. Anna Donovan

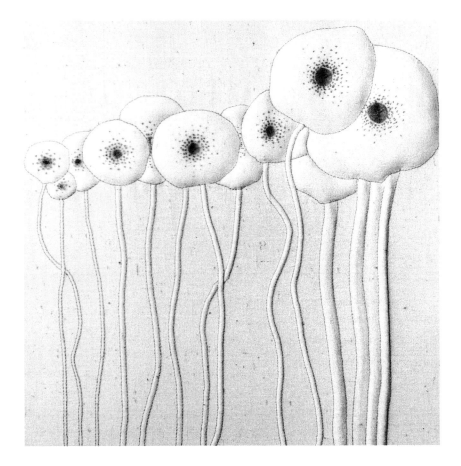

as shadow work. The most important factor is, of course, safety. Otherwise, like all the materials which can be used for the other forms of quilting, washability, workability and suitability have to be considered.

## Method of stuffed quilting

Two layers of fabric are required – the front and the backing. They should be properly ironed before use, because they cannot be ironed after the quilting.

As there is likely to be a good deal of manoeuvring round the design, fit the transparent appliqué foot, since the pattern lines will show through it. Also, being short-fronted, it takes up less space in the work and is easy to move about.

- Using one of the methods described in Chapter 1, transfer the design to the right side of the layer to be stitched.

- Pin and tack the front and backing fabrics together with right sides facing.
- Set the machine for a medium-length straight stitch and adjust top and bobbin tensions to suit the threads.
- Start stitching as near the centre as is practical and work round the motifs which are to be stuffed. Finish the stitching completely before beginning any filling of shapes. It is very difficult to stitch round a design when it has been partially quilted. Every so often, take the thread ends through to the back, and tie and cut them off; if they are allowed to accumulate they will only tangle and obstruct the machining.
- When all the stitching is completed, and the ends of threads finished off at the back, the outlined motifs are ready to be filled.
- If the backing fabric is a loosely-woven one, gently ease apart the fibres with the stuffing stick to make a small gap to push the filling through (see Fig 107).
- Using the stuffing stick, push in the filling in small amounts at a time. While the cavity must be completely filled to a well-rounded form, it must not be over-stuffed – hard lumpy quilting is not in any way attractive.
- Check the front frequently to make sure that each motif is evenly padded, with no empty 'pouches', and that it is not lumpy, or too hard and over-stuffed.
- When the motif is properly filled, close the gap by easing the separated fibres together again (see Fig 108).
- With a firm closely-woven backing material, the fibres cannot be eased apart for filling. Instead, make a little slit with sharp-pointed scissors (see Fig 109). Do not make the slit too large as it can fray and stretch, and grow with pushing in the filling.
- Fill the shape as before, and oversew the gap by hand to close (see Fig 110).

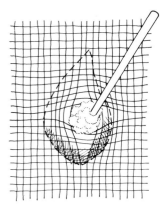

**107** The back of the stitched outline of a motif with the filling being inserted between separated threads

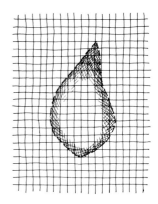

**108** The separated threads eased together after filling

When filling large shapes it is practical to make several stuffing gaps, or holes, rather than one large one.

The choice of stitching for motifs to be filled is wide, but depends mainly on the capability of the machine and its operator. It could be running, zig-zag, satin or free-motion stitchery worked with a single needle; double or triple needle stitching; or else a fancy automatic stitch. But it must be said that free-motion stitching will finish this stage in a fraction of the time taken by the other methods.

Additional interest and texture can be created by stitching the flat background areas from which the padded mounds stand proud. Why not include some machine or hand embroidery embellished with beads to give the piece extra lift? Any work to the background must, of course, be done before outlining the motifs, certainly before any suggestion of stuffing.

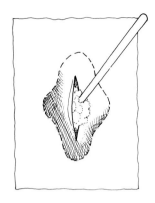

**109** Insertion of the filling through a narrow slit cut at the back

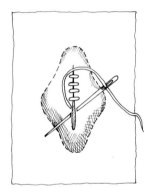

**110** Over-sewing the slit opening to close after filling

**111** (above right) Shadow quilted stuffed shapes and corded lines worked with double needle on polyester jersey. Anne Hulbert

**112** (right) The reverse of Fig 111 showing the quilted shapes and lines with stuffing gaps closed by oversewing. Anne Hulbert

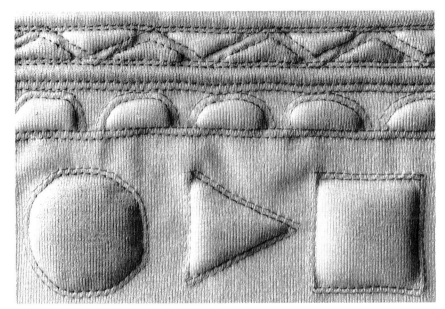

**113** *Green Leaves.* Tied-and-dyed panel in soft cotton. Design was outlined with a silver thread couched on with a narrow zig-zag stitch. Wadding and backing fabric were cut away at the back, leaving only the motifs padded and raised high above a very flat, unquilted background. 38cm by 48cm (15in by 19in). Anne Hulbert

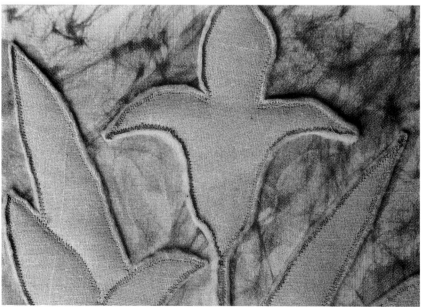

**114** The flat unquilted reverse of *Green Leaves* (Fig 113) showing how the backing and wadding have been cut away from the background, leaving only the motifs padded. Anne Hulbert

## Mock trapunto

This is a quick way of padding and raising a motif higher than its background. It is sometimes referred to as 'fake' or padded trapunto. The method can be seen in the photographs of 'Green Leaves' (Figs 113 and 114) which show the front and the reverse of the work.

- Cut out a piece of wadding and a piece of backing fabric, both about 5cm (2in) larger all round than the motif to be padded.
- Tack them together to the back of the motif with the wadding sandwiched in the middle.
- Stitch, in a small to medium zig-zag, all round the outline of the motif, through all three layers.
- Now, leaving the front intact, cut away the excess wadding and backing behind the motif – as close as possible to the stitching without damaging either the stitches or the front fabric.
- Remove the tacking stitches.

**115** *Clementina*. Cushion front. Flowers and leaves printed on a furnishing linen-union were outlined with free-motion stitching and raised with stuffed quilting. A form of log-cabin patchwork frames the design. Anne Hulbert

Very small and complicated patterns are not feasible for this type of quilting. Manoeuvring sharp-pointed scissors to cut out intricate outlines is difficult; and dangerous, too, for the front fabric!

Mock trapunto is a good technique for pictures and hangings where a high relief might be required, especially if a firm 'foam' is used instead of the lighter wadding. If the finished project is mounted and stretched tightly over a piece of plywood, the padded areas will be thrown up very high indeed. The sides of the front material should be taken round the back and laced together tightly to keep the work taut.

**116** Sketch for a small picture for working in stuffed and corded shadow quilting

**117** *Dry Tree, Goonhilly,* Cornwall. An interesting design for incorporating stuffed corded quilting methods

**118** Tulip shape outlined on lawn-backed calico with triple needle stitching in three shades of red and pink. Filled with chopped scraps of polyester wadding. Anne Hulbert

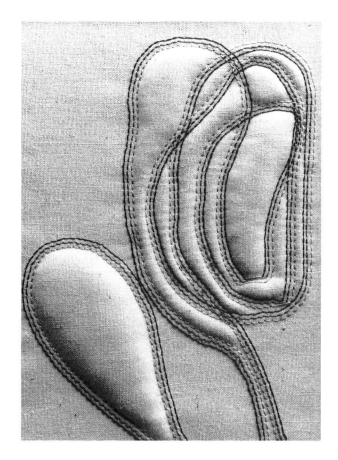

**119** Stuffed shadow quilting with fine voile on calico. (Work in progress.) Geometric shapes outlined with double needle stitching and filled variously with glass and metallic beads and bugle, and cotton fibres and cut wool. Anne Hulbert

**120** (top left) Design for stuffed shadow-quilting for the top of a silk-covered trinket box

**121** (top right) Suggestion for a cushion front. Stuffed centre design worked on a background of random stitched wadded quilting with thick, but softly padded borders

**122** (left) A Victorian tile pattern suitable for a pocket, box-lid or stool-top using stuffed and other quilting methods in the same project

**123** Ideas from various sources for stuffed quilting. Intricate patterns can always be done with free-motion stitching

**124** *Walls of Avila, Spain.* A fine subject for the basis of a stuffed quilted picture, perhaps in watercolour painted on silk

**125** *Fruit harvest*. Cushion front. Stuffed quilting on a heavy furnishing cotton with a calico backing. The design was outlined with free-motion stitching. Anne Hulbert

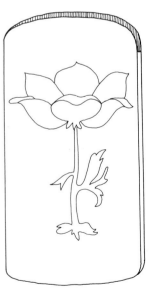

**126** Stuffed quilting design for a soft leather spectacle case

**127** Classic designs, from various sources, suitable for stuffed quilting

# CHAPTER 9

# Shadow Quilting

Delicate, softly-coloured 'shadows' can be created by sandwiching a coloured filling between a transparent top fabric and its backing. Shadow work can be incorporated into all methods of quilting, providing further interest to a project. Corded and stuffed quilting, for instance, where the fillings are inserted from the back, are worked in the manner described in earlier chapters, but varied by using coloured fillings behind fine materials.

Among the many transparent fabrics suitable for the front are silk, habutai, chiffon, net, organdie, voile and muslin. For corded shadow work, interesting fillings to use are knitting yarn, tapisserie wool, leather and plastic thonging, threaded beads and strips of printed

**128** Suggestions for shadow quilting from Japanese crest designs.

fabric. For stuffed shadow work, fillings of chopped fabrics and wools, loose beads, bright sequins, hair, seeds and grain can provide unusual and attractive effects.

A quite different form of shadow quilting can be produced with fillings of flat, low-fraying materials like felt, leather, plastic, painted Vilene, closely woven printed fabrics and even tinsel paper. For this technique, since it is not possible to insert the filling from the back, the felt (for example) is applied to the backing fabric, covered with a layer of transparent fabric and stitched around to secure it. This method will produce a uniformly flat motif without the rounded contours arising from filling pattern shapes from the back.

Designs for shadow quilting with flat pattern shapes must be kept simple with clear uncomplicated outlines. Stencil-type designs are ideal; the spaces round the sections could be used for lines of stitching.

The purpose of shadow quilting is mainly decorative – it can be used for fabric pictures and hangings, box lids and articles unlikely to suffer much handling.

**129** Pineapple stencil to develop for shadow quilting with a low-fray fabric. Colour Vilene shapes to resemble the 'scales', and decorate with glass beads and hand embroidery. Cover with a transparent fabric and secure with stitching in a trellis pattern

**130** *Contemplation.* The figure was cut from black felt, and the 'rock' and shaded areas from three layers of black chiffon. They were applied to a background of white silk and decorated with lines of metallic gold stitching, tiny strips of gold kid and small gold beads. The work was then overlaid with a layer of black chiffon and each section stitched all round with narrow zig-zag. 36cm by 50cm (14in by 20in). Anna Donovan

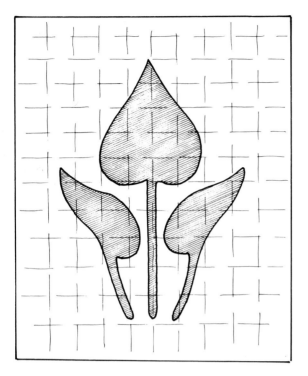

**131** (left) The felt pieces of the design tacked vertically and horizontally to the backing fabric

**132** (below left) The transparent top fabric tacked diagonally over the secured felt pieces

**133** (below) The finished work with the stitching round the motifs completed and the tackings removed

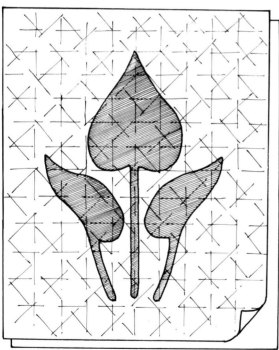

## Method for shadow-quilting with felt and low-fray materials

- Transfer the design to the felt and cut out all pattern pieces.
- Lay them on the inside of the piece of backing and tack each in place, in vertical and horizontal lines, leaving enough space in between for stitching one or more rows as required (see Fig 131). They can be glued in place, but only very lightly, or the glue may seep through the fabrics.
- Place the top transparent fabric, right side up, over the applied felt pieces and tack down diagonally (see Fig 132).
- Stitch round the outline pattern shapes – i.e. only through the top and backing fabrics (see also Fig 132). Straight stitch is often used, but the work can be greatly enhanced by using zig-zag, or any of the automatic stitches the machine has to offer. Couching thicker threads between the motifs could add exciting textural detail to contrast with the flatness of the design, but too much intricacy in the design is best avoided.
- Remove all tacking stitches (see Fig 133).

The depth of colour in shadow-quilted designs is entirely governed by the thickness of the top fabric used to cover the designs. The more transparent the fabric, the stronger and clearer the colour, texture and outline of the design and its filling will appear.

# C H A P T E R 10

# Padded Work

The book would be incomplete without a few words about padded work. At its simplest, it merely involves filling out likely-looking shapes which are acceptable in a flat and unpadded state, but which are immeasurably improved by being softly 'plumped up' with filling. Such work, by its nature, relates beautifully to quilting, and can greatly enrich it.

**Example**

*A padded pompon* (see Fig 134)

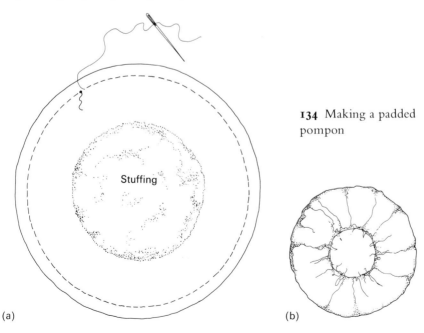

**134** Making a padded pompon

Stuffing

(a)                                    (b)

**135** A selection of padded and quilted articles and motifs. The bird, heart needle-case, leaves and flowers were quilted with free-stitching through the wadding, before making up and finishing with cut-work edges. The pot-holder was patched and quilted, and the edges were bound with bias strips. The wadded fronts of the heart and shell pincushions were stencilled, spray-dyed, quilted and beaded prior to making them up. In the centre, a padded pompon. Anne Hulbert and others

Pompons can be used for many decorative articles, including flowers, rosettes, and 'eyes'. To make:

(a) Cut a circle of fabric twice the diameter of the required finished pompon. Run a gathering thread round the edge. Place a knob of filling in the centre, sufficient to fill the pompon softly when drawn up. Draw up tightly to enclose the filling, and to close the gap. Fasten off.
(b) The finished pompon. These can be made in any size, and in most materials that will gather easily.

**Cut-work** (see Fig 136)
This is an ideal method for producing free-standing padded motifs, and it can be worked on any swing-needle sewing machine. Detached motifs can give life to an ordinary piece of quilting, adding movement and a sense of reality. Although they are made as separate pieces, they can be temporarily attached to a design in different ways:

(a)

(b)

(c)

(i) with a few stitches in the centre; (ii) by attaching press studs; or (iii) by sewing a safety-pin to the back, as a brooch. Thin cord or fine wire can be couched round the edges by the stitching; cord serves as a stiffener, and wire allows the motif to be manipulated into a more natural shape. To make:

(a) Mark the design outline on the top fabric and tack it to a layer of backing material, with a layer of wadding, if required, sandwiched between them. The materials should be about 2.5cm (1in) larger all round than the motif, to provide room for holding the work while stitching.

(b) Stitch round the outline in a narrow and fairly close zig-zag: start by experimenting with a stitch width setting of no. 2 and a stitch length setting of no. 2. Reduce both settings for very small motifs. Any inside markings, like petal lines and leaf veining, should be quilted at this stage.

(c) Cut away the excess layers of materials very close to the zig-zag without cutting the stitches. If necessary, tack on a lining at this

**136** Working cut-work

**137** Little girl's cream dress and hat decorated with lavender and blue cut-work quilted silk flowers. The armholes, waist and hemline of the dress were flat quilted with fancy automatic machine stitching. Anna Donovan

stage to cover the back of the inner quilting. Work all round the edges in close satin stitch – use a higher width setting and a shorter stitch length to ensure the first round of zig-zag stitches is covered for neatness. For a really good finish to the edge keep the central groove of the presser foot on the edge of the motif. Perfecting this method of finishing edges is a great advantage – any manner of free-standing motif can be used as an extra decoration. It is also much used for machine appliqué.

## Appliqué and padded appliqué

Appliqué is the method by which cut-out shapes of fabric are applied to a background material to form a design. The shapes are secured by satin or zig-zag stitching, which is a quick and easy operation on the sewing machine. This form of decoration, with its ability to enrich an otherwise plain design, has great appeal. The pieces to be appliquéd may first be sprayed, painted, embroidered or beaded; or they can be elements of the design cut from a printed fabric. There are two methods of appliqué in machine quilting.

### Iron-on bonding

This involves using an iron-on bonding material to apply the unpadded motif to the top fabric before quilting. One side of the bonding feels a little rough, and the other has the feel of greaseproof paper. The adhesive is activated by the heat of the iron. Although it adds a slight stiffness to the applied motif, its use does stop the raw edges from fraying – no more edges to be turned under.

- Place the wrong side of the fabric on to the rough side of the bonding and cut out both together, so that they are exactly the same size and shape.
- Iron them together with the temperature set to suit the top fabric. When cold peel off the paper backing – the back of the motif will now feel slightly tacky. Place it wrong side down on the right side of the background material and iron well to secure it.
- Stitch all round the edge of the motif with zig-zag or satin stitch. If the background fabric is tacked to wadding and backing materials before the stitching is worked, the appliquéd motif will be quilted.

## Padded appliqué

Follow stages (a) and (b) of the instructions for cut-work (Fig 136). When the motif has been cut out close to the stitching of the first round of zig-zag, tack it to the right side of the background fabric. Use a close zig-zag or satin stitch and stitch all round the edges, covering the first round. When applied to a flat background the padded motif is well raised. However, it can be further plumped up by leaving a small gap in the stitching and pushing in extra stuffing.

## Examples

*Padded flowers* (see Fig 138)

It is quick and easy to make this type of flower as a free-standing motif – or one that can be stitched to a background, round its centre, leaving the petals free. It can be cut from a printed fabric, or from a dyed or painted plain fabric. To make:

(a)  Place two layers of fabric together with wrong sides facing. Mark, tack and stitch the petal shape as shown.

(b)  Turn to the right side and insert a piece of wadding cut to the same shape and size. Pin two tucks in the petal. Make four more petals to match.

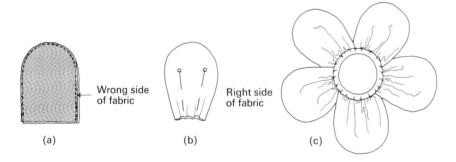

Wrong side
of fabric

Right side
of fabric

(a)　　　　　　　　(b)　　　　　　　(c)

**138** (left) A padded flower

**139** (above) *Garden Flowers* – this beautiful carved wood wall-panel is an inspiration for creating an arrangement in similar style with dyed silks. Try using padded and quilted flowers and leaves, with beads and machine embroidery. Height 60cm (24in). Valerie Hadley

(c)  Cut a circle of fabric for the centre. Tack the petals at evenly spaced intervals to the wrong side of the circle, and zig-zag round the edge to secure each petal. Place the completed flower, with a knob of stuffing behind the centre, on its fabric background and satin stitch all round the centre, through all layers, to secure it, leaving the petals free. For a totally separate flower (instead of one stitched to a background) cut a second circle of fabric for the centre, tack it to the back and include it in the round of satin stitch.

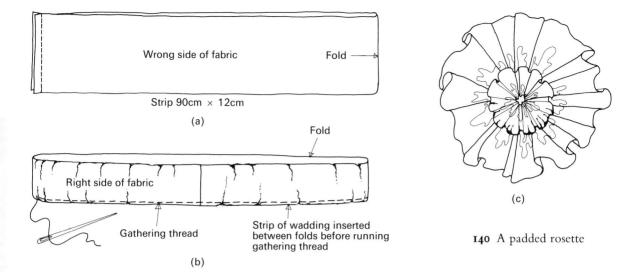

Wrong side of fabric      Fold ⟶

Strip 90cm × 12cm

(a)

Fold

Right side of fabric

Gathering thread

Strip of wadding inserted
between folds before running
gathering thread

(b)

(c)

**140** A padded rosette

*Padded rosette* (see Fig 140)

Rosettes are now much used with soft furnishings, and add a touch of luxury, but padded rosettes are even more striking. To make:

(a) Cut a strip of fabric 90cm (36in) long and 12cm (5in) wide. Stitch the ends together with right sides facing.

(b) Turn the wrong side over to the inside to make a double cuff-like shape, so only the right sides now show. Cut a strip of wadding slightly smaller than the 'cuff' and slide it between the folds. Run a gathering thread all round the raw edges, through the three layers.

(c) Pull up tight and fasten off. Cover the gap in the centre with a smaller pompon and/or several beads.

*'Pad-as-you-go'* (see Fig 141)

This is really quite an old method of making warm bedcovers, but it can be a most useful technique for making a variety of other articles. The pockets for the wadding and the wadding itself are put together at the same time, with no stitching showing on the right side, rather in the way that some duvets are made. To make:

(a) Cut out a backing piece of fabric. Cut a strip of top fabric and, with right side uppermost, tack one side of it (1) to the bottom of the backing. Cut a strip of wadding slightly smaller than the strip of top fabric; omit the seam allowances. Lay the wadding along

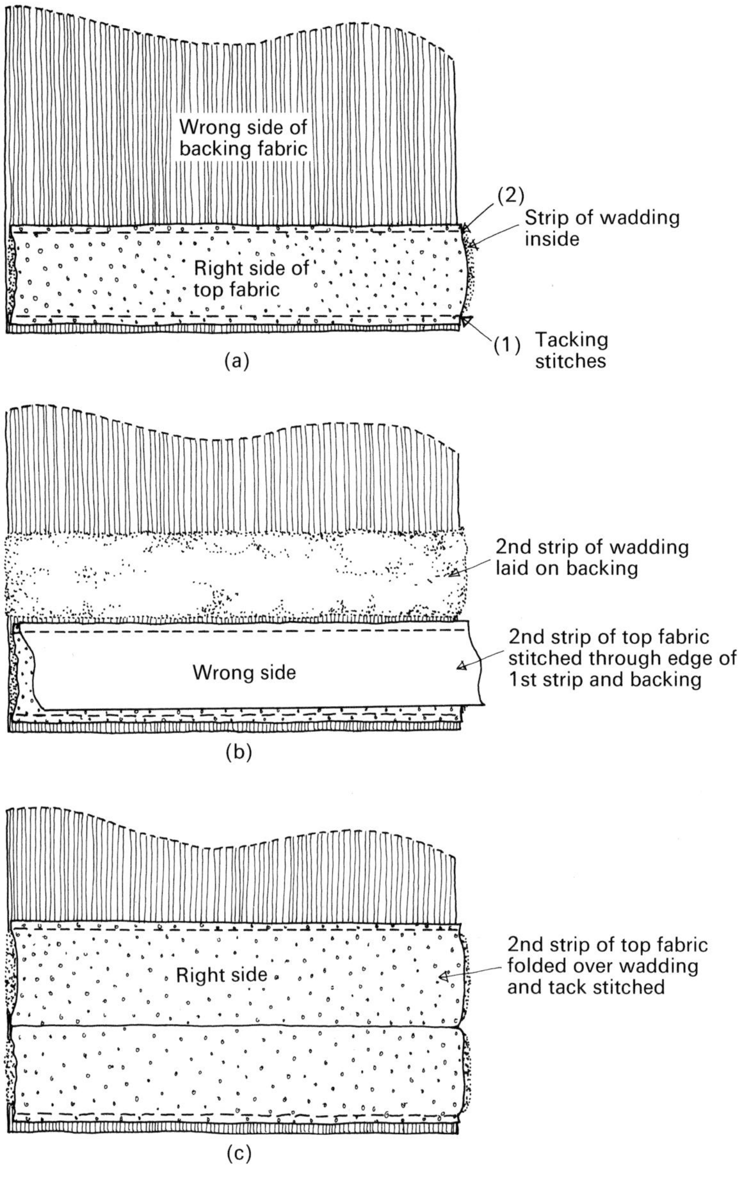

Wrong side of
backing fabric

(2)
Strip of wadding
inside

Right side of
top fabric

(1) Tacking
stitches

(a)

2nd strip of wadding
laid on backing

2nd strip of top fabric
stitched through edge of
1st strip and backing

Wrong side

(b)

2nd strip of top fabric
folded over wadding
and tack stitched

Right side

(c)

the backing underneath the piece of top fabric already tacked on.
Tack along the other edge of the top fabric (2) as shown, but do
not catch the wadding in the stitching.

(b) Cut another strip of top fabric and place it, with right sides
facing, on to the first strip and stitch along the edge through to
the backing. Cut another strip of wadding and place it on the
backing.

**142** Shoe tea-cosy. Silk satin with wadded quilting in free-motion stitchery, and satin stitch for the window. The roof material was flat quilted with free stitching. Kim Clarke

(c) Fold the second strip of top fabric over the wadding and tack it down. Continue stitching the strips of top fabric to the previous one to hide the stitching, folding each over a strip of wadding until the area is covered with softly padded rows.

Although 'pad–as–you–go' designs are based on straight lines, quite a variety of pattern can be produced. In particular, strip patchwork patterns make an interesting variation.

**143** *Summer Time*, in blues and greens. Machine knitted child's slipover with wadded quilting along the 'waves'. The teddy bears were made by stuffing knitted pieces. Hand-embroidered faces. Nicky Mills

**144** Random quilted silk pincushion, spray-dyed and stencilled silk bag, and painted free-standing silk flowers and butterflies. All finished with hand embroidery, and sequins and glass beads. Pinks and greens. Sue Rangeley

# The Finishing Touches

The appearance of a good piece of quilting can easily be ruined by an ill-chosen style of finish. It must above all be compatible with the work – through its colour, pattern and texture, or through the technique used in producing it. The essential criteria for an edging, border or trimming are that it should relate to, embellish and complete the work, as well as emphasize its beauty. The finishes are vital – here are some suggestions.

## Edgings to add to the outside of a finished seam.

**Twisted cord** (see Fig 145)
Silk, cotton, rayon and metallic cords are available in different thicknesses. To apply to an edge, leave a small gap in the seam stitching and tuck the end of the cord into it. Stitch the cord to the seam as shown. Tuck the finishing end into the gap with the other end, stitch the gap to close and secure the ends of cord.

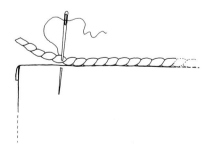

**145** Twisted cord

## Rouleau (see Fig 146)

A rouleau is a hollow tube of fabric stitched on the wrong side and turned to right side. It resembles a shoelace and its use can be very decorative. It is shown stitched to the seam at intervals to form loops along the edge of the work.

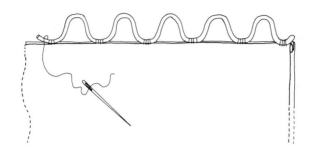

**146** Rouleau

## Ric-rac braid (see Fig 147)

This is inexpensive and can be bought at most haberdashery counters. Ric-rac is easily gathered along the centre, and drawn up to make a pretty ruched trimming.

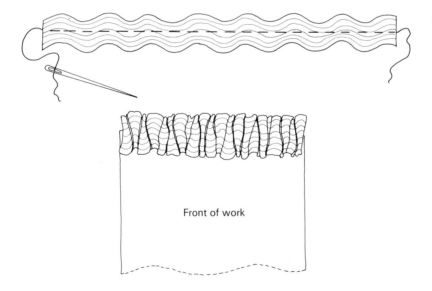

**147** Ric-rac braid

Front of work

## Padded plait (see Fig 148)

The 'strands' are padded hollow tubes of fabric and may be of any thickness from a fine rouleau to something plump and bulky. To

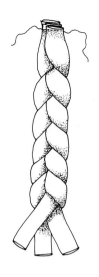

make the plait, first make three fabric tubes and turn right side out. Insert the filling – a soft yarn can be drawn through thinner tubes, and fat tubes can be stuffed with strips of wadding or loose synthetic filling. Stitch the ends of the padded tubes of fabric together as shown and plait them together.

**Binding a seam** (see Fig 149)
When layers of material are too bulky to join on the wrong side and turn smoothly to the right side, they can instead be stitched on the right side and neatly bound to cover the raw edges.

Stitch a bias cut strip of fabric to the front edge of the work with right sides facing. Turn under the raw edge along the other side of the bias strip and fold it over to the back. Hand stitch along the edge, just covering the line of machine stitches. This type of treatment to the edge of work can be attractively decorated with fancy automatic stitches.

**148** Padded plait

**149** (below) Binding a seam

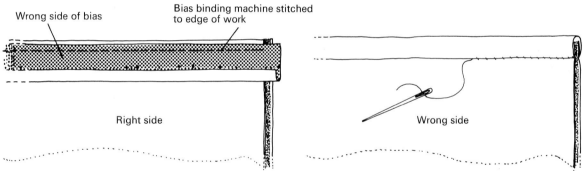

Wrong side of bias

Bias binding machine stitched to edge of work

Right side

Wrong side

## Edgings to be stitched within the seam allowance

**Knotted trellis** (see Fig 150)
Tie neat knots in the centres of strips of rouleau. The length depends on the width of the edging required, making allowance for the knots. Stitch the pieces to a length of narrow tape as shown, so that each one

**150** Knotted trellis

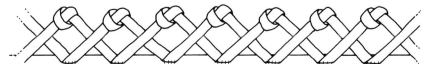

half overlaps the one before. Stitching them to tape secures the pieces, making them more manageable.

For a cushion, tack and stitch the taped edge to the raw edge on the front of the work, with all the knots pointing inwards towards the centre of the cushion. Tack and stitch the back piece of the cushion to the front with right sides facing, including (and also concealing) the taped edge of the knotted trellis in the seam. Turn the work to the right side, and the result will be a delightful border framing the work.

**Triangles from folded squares** (see Fig 151)
Although there are four thicknesses of fabric to each triangle, this is a very decorative border, and of course the fabric can be as light and delicate as desired. Fold, say, 10cm (4in) squares of material diagonally in half, then diagonally in half again to make triangles $75 \times 75 \times 100$mm ($3 \times 3 \times 4$in). Tack them together along the raw edges. Then tack and stitch them in with the seam round the edge of the work.

**151** Folded triangles

**Piping** (see Fig 152)
Piping is simply a length of fabric-covered cord for inserting into a seam to give a neat finish to an edge. The fabric is usually cut on the bias (diagonally across the grain) and the cord can vary in thickness to make a thicker or thinner finish to an edge.

(a) Fold the fabric to find the bias across the straight grain.

(b) Mark lines parallel to the fold as shown, and cut into strips. The width of the strips must be the width of the required bias strip plus seam allowances on both edges.

(c) Join the strips, when necessary, as shown, with little triangles overlapping at the corners to ensure a continuous straight edge over the join. Iron the seam out flat and trim off the bits.

(d) Fold the fabric strip in half lengthwise over the piping cord and tack through, as close as possible to the cord.

**152** Piping

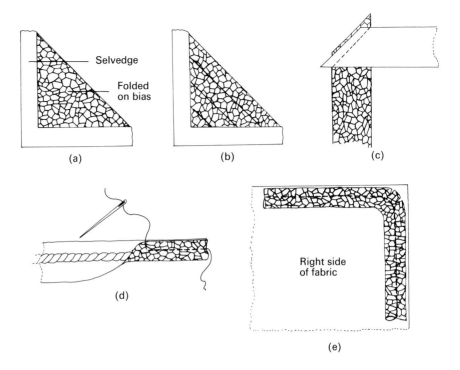

Selvedge

Folded on bias

(a)

(b)

(c)

(d)

Right side of fabric

(e)

(e) Pin and tack the piping on to the right side of the front of the work as shown, snipping the corners to enable it to negotiate the bend. Then lay the back piece, right side facing the front, and tack and stitch all round through all layers and very close to the enclosed piping.

A pretty, out-of-the-ordinary piping can be made by using a near-transparent silk to cover a coloured thick, soft yarn instead of the traditional cord.

### Gathered frills (see Fig 153)

Gathering can be done by machine with a maximum length of straight stitch and a loosened top tension. Use a strong thread and make two rows of stitching. Pull up the two bobbin threads to gather the fabric – do not pull up the top threads as they will tighten, and lock the bobbin threads, with the risk of breaking. Some machines have a small gathering foot which is useful for lightweight fabrics. Some can accommodate the hefty 'ruffler', a large and somewhat noisy contraption, excellent for making a pleated, rather than a gathered frill. It can be adjusted to make pleats of different widths.

Frills are smarter and crisper made with double fabric. For good fullness, allow double the length of the edges to which the frill is to be

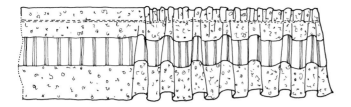

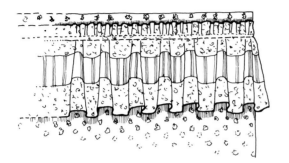

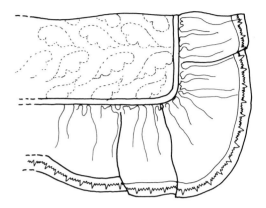

attached. Some quite imaginative frills can be invented, as shown in the diagram. Try making them from joined strips of fabric; add fancy stitching; or cord-quilt them for extra stiffness.

**153** Gathered frills

Tack the gathered frill to the right side of the front of the work, matching the raw edges. Tack the back piece over them, with the right side facing inwards. Tack and stitch all layers together with the frill sandwiched in the seam.

## Log cabin framing (see Fig 154)
Padded log cabin patchwork can be used successfully as a frame for quilted pictures, and to surround a design on a cushion. The quilted area looks quite striking with surrounding bands of fabric in toning colours. Stitch the border pieces round the quilted design, in the order shown, with a strip of wadding under each in the 'pad-as-you-go' fashion.

## Decorative bows (see Fig 155)
Bows are very much in vogue, and exhibit a wide choice in their styles. The bows shown would be made from stitched tubes of fabric. The tailored bow needs a strip of fabric twice the length of the finished bow, plus a short length to fold round for the knot. Fold the

**154** Log cabin framing

strip in half lengthwise and stitch across it just under halfway from the cut ends. Take the centre of the fold back to the line of stitches and tack them together. Fold the short piece of fabric round the centre of the bow, covering the tacking and stitching. Stitch one end and then the other end of the knot to the back of the bow to secure.

The other bow is softer and fuller, and requires much more material. It can be made using the same principles as the tailored bow, but with considerably longer tails; or simply tied by the 'shoelace' method. Both styles of bow would look more luxuriant if padded with wadding.

**155** Decorative bows

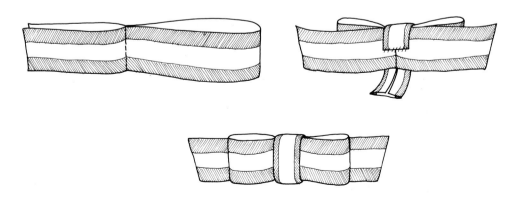

# Suppliers of Materials and Equipment

The following materials and equipment were used for the articles that appear in this book. They are generally available from needlework shops, large department stores, craft shops, art shops and hardware stores.

Calico, muslin, polycotton; sheet wadding (batting); synthetic (toy) filling; Bondaweb and Vilene interfacings; silk twill, habutai, antung and satin.

Wonder (wash-out) marker; Vogart transfer pencil; Dewhurst Tailor's Chalk; Milward's tracing wheel; Briggs embroidery transfers; Butterick dressmaker's carbon.

Madeira rayon, cotton and metallic threads; Gutterman polyester, metallic and cotton threads; Coates Drima, Dual Duty, Chain, Effektgarn (metallic), Super Sheen threads; Coates/Anchor tapisserie wool; stranded cotton, pearl cotton, Mercer crochet cotton, Astrella and Zierlitze (couching) threads; Molnlyncke Spun Syntet and Goliath; Offray ribbons.

Badger air brushes; Air-tex textile paints; Dylon fabric dyes, Color-fun and dye sticks; Deka textile paints; Rowney fabric dyes, Pelikan textile paints; CarPlan spray paints; Pentel permanent markers; Edding metallic permanent markers.

*The following companies offer a mail order service.*

Beckfoot Mill, Prince Street, Dudley Hill, Bradford BD4 6HQ.
    Safe wadding/batting & synthetic fillings.
Wm H. Bennett & Sons, 79 Piccadilly, Manchester M1 2BX.
    Silk habutai, satin, twill & antung, etc.

Ells and Farrier, 5 Princes Street, London W1.
  Glass, pearl, metal & plastic beads, drops and sequins.
John Lewis & Co. Ltd, Oxford Street, London W1R 1EX.
  A wide section of fabrics, beads, quilting materials and
  sewing accessories.
Liberty & Co. Ltd, Regent Street, London W1A 1EX.
  A wide selection of fabrics, including silks, leathers and
  suedes.
Lowe and Carr Ltd, Coniston Avenue, Leicester LE2 7FJ.
  Transfer pencils for use on natural fibres only, e.g. cotton,
  linen, etc.
MacCulloch & Wallis, 25–26 Dering Street, London W1R 0BH.
  Muslin, domette, wadding, silk, calico, lining, interlining,
  cotton, rayon and velvet. Also threads, cords and a wide
  range of sewing accessories.
Mace and Nairn, 89 Crane Street, Salisbury, Wiltshire.
  Fabrics and sewing requisites.
Mulberry Silks, Unit 12A, Worcester Road Industrial Estate,
  Chipping Norton, Oxon OX7 5XW.
  Hand-dyed fine & medium silk threads.
Patchwork Cat & Calico Dog, 21 Chalk Farm Road, London
  NW1.
  All quilting supplies.
Pioneer Patches, Marsh Mills, Lucklane, Huddersfield HD3 4AB.
  Quilting supplies and printed patterns.
Russell & Chapple, 23 Monmouth Street, London, WC2H 9DE.
  Art canvas, drill and cotton duck.
The Prideaux Collection, Vivien Prideaux, Towan Textiles,
  Trevilla, Feock, Truro, Cornwall TR3 6QG.
  Individually hand-dyed silk threads. Textiles, machine
  embroidery and quilting courses are held regularly at the
  Towan Textile Workshops. Brochures available from the
  above address.
George Weil & Sons, The Warehouse, Reading Arch Road,
  Redhill, Surrey RH1 1HG.
  A wide variety of silk and cotton fabrics, dyes and paints,
  and equipment for textile colouring.


A Bernina sewing machine was used for all the machine work by
the author, and for much of the work by the contributors.
Enquiries to the Bernina Distributors, The Bogod Machine Co.
Ltd, 50–52 Great Sutton Street, London EC1V 0DJ.

# Bibliography

Virginia Avery, *Quilts to Wear*, Unwin Hyman, 1982

Muriel Best, *Stumpwork*, Batsford 1987

Pauline Brown, *Embroidery Backgrounds – Painting and Dyeing Techniques*, Batsford 1984

Anne Butler, *Machine Stitches*, Batsford 1976

Valerie Campbell-Harding and Pamela Watts, *Machine Embroidery–Stitch Techniques*, Batsford 1989

Averil Colby, *Quilting*, Batsford 1972

Anne Coleman, *The Creative Sewing Machine*, Batsford 1979

Carolyn Hall, *The Sewing Machine Craft Book*, Van Nostrand Reinhold Co. 1980

Jennifer Gray, *Machine Embroidery*, Batsford 1973

Moyra McNeill, *Machine Embroidery – Lace and See-through Techniques*, Batsford 1985

Gloria Ramsey, *Couching – Decorative Laid Thread Embroidery*, Batsford 1976

Christine Risley, *Machine Embroidery*, Studio Vista 1973

Eirian Short, *Quilting – Technique, Design and Application*, Batsford 1974

In addition, Dover Publications Inc, New York, and Constable & Co, publish a very wide and enlightening range of paperbacks with examples of almost every aspect of world-wide art, crafts, and design. Amateurs and professional needleworkers alike are sure to find much inspiration among their splendid collections of authentic designs. These books are sold in book shops and art supplies shops.

# INDEX